TROUPER COOPER'S CURRY COOKBOOK

By the same author
The Parnell Cookbook

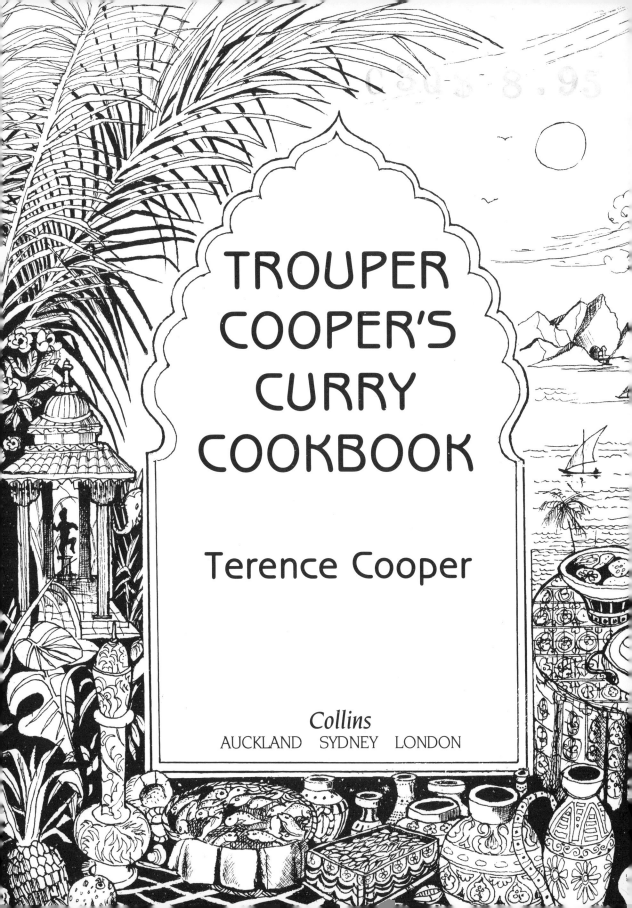

TROUPER COOPER'S CURRY COOKBOOK

Terence Cooper

Collins
AUCKLAND   SYDNEY   LONDON

FOR LYN
who tasted them all
and survived

First published 1982
Reprinted 1982
William Collins Publishers Ltd
P.O. Box 1, Auckland

© 1982 Terence Cooper

ISBN 0 00 216994 0

Typeset by Jacobson Typesetters, Auckland
Printed in Hong Kong

CONTENTS

Sepoys from the Madras Pioneers and the Queen's Own Corps of Guides

INTRODUCTION

I have had a love affair with Indian cooking ever since I tasted my first curry, and I have no hesitation in stating that it's addictive. I can only thank any of the multitudes of gods that it is not a criminal addiction, although some of my friends who suffered my early attempts at curry claimed that I was culpable of assault with a deadly dish. However, 'Omnia vinces perseverando' was the motto on the cap badge of one of the schools I was subjected to, and I applied it. Not out of any respect for the protestant work ethic, but out of love.

All food is hedged about by myths and fictions sedulously propogated by earnest experts of one sort or another. Forlorn groups of bewildered people are commanded to evenings of ethnic food, where they are bombarded with curious vegetables, odd cuts of meat and suspect sauces. Arcane vocabularies and phrases abound, and I remember when I frequented such gatherings I burnished my words with the best.

I still recall the look of horror on the visage of the vicar's wife when I upbraided those who piddled with their food. She, of course, took it in the dictionary sense ('to make water, now vulgar'), but I had discovered that it also meant to peck at your food, to pick and trifle with it — as did Jacobean character Simon Tanner in Thomas Middleton's play *The Mayor of Quinborough* when he demanded dinner:

Give order that twelve pigs be roasted yellow,
Nine geese and some three larks for piddling meat, and twenty woodcocks.

Nevertheless, these attitudes and conceits gave early members of the 'Brown Windsor brigade' plenty of ammunition with which to abuse 'all that foreign muck', and none more so than curry.

LIST OF MYTHS AND FICTIONS PERTAINING TO CURRY
as promoted by the 'Brown Windsor Brigade'

1. Curry is a mysterious eastern revenge on Europeans.
2. Curry is designed to disguise rotten ingredients.
3. Curry is better the hotter it is.
4. Curry creates dyspepsia.
5. Curry fosters an evil temper.
6. Curry is a sort of stew with curry powder in it.

I use the word 'curry' rather than curries, because many unfortunates refer to it as if it were a specific dish, an attitude fostered by establishments that feature 'curry and rice' on their menus, occasionally qualified by what is actually curried, viz sausages. There are, of course, literally hundreds of curries: wet, dry, sweet, sour, created with flesh, fowl, or fish. There are purely vegetarian dishes, and many may be devoted solely to lentils, peas or beans, eggs or aubergines. In fact Indian cooking has probably more vegetarian variations than any other cuisine. Food is also barbecued, roasted, baked and deep fried. But it's all spicy and it ain't necessarily hot. Heat is *not* an essential characteristic, and excessive use of chilli is the hallmark of an unimaginative cook. Certainly there is heat in some dishes, but it should never be harsh or fierce.

The origin of the word curry is obscure, but the most popular interpretation is that it's the anglicised version of 'kari', a Tamil word from southern India meaning sauce. Possibly a more accurate meaning is that it's any combination of spices used in cooking.

Because of the incredible complexity of Indian society, there's really no technique or style of cooking that could properly be called a national cuisine. The universal observance of religious and caste restrictions makes it impossible. The vast majority of Indians are Hindus and therefore vegetarian, but almost every Hindu has his own idea of what a vegetarian is. The ancient sacred books of the Hindus — the Vedas, the Upanishads and the Sastras — devote considerable care to the subject of food, and the rules they laid down have been observed through the centuries to become an intrinsic part of the Hindu way of life.

Other reasons for the great diversity of Indian cooking are the influences exerted by the extremes of climate and terrain. In a land that has snow-capped mountains, arid deserts, vast plains and steaming deltas, the amount and variety of natural raw materials, and consequently the culinary methods of using them, is enormous.

Despite the rapid development of urban areas, India is still an agricultural sub-continent very dependent on the climate, and there is one climatic feature that dominates everything — the monsoon. Dams, tube wells, and irrigation schemes are changing the old agricultural pattern, but the food supply of the sub-continent is still an annual gamble with the monsoon. Nowhere is the expression 'feast or famine' more poignant.

Food found in southern India is the hottest and spiciest of the sub-continent, and basically vegetarian. The coconut palm, (called the 'tree of wealth' because you can use every part of it) grows in every back yard, so coconut grated, in chunks, or in the form of oil, features in nearly every dish. Meals often begin and end with rice, for the vegetarians of the south have great respect for rice. They choose, with enormous care, the particular kind of rice they need: long-grained basumati for pilaus, round rice for sweets; polished rice and partly husked rice for some dishes, glutinous rice for others. Their rice comes pressed, pounded, puffed, or ground; they have rice flour too. The south is also the land of mar-vellous tropical fruits and the coffee here is superb.

The Punjab in the north is the great wheat basket of India, so breads rather than rice are a staple of this region, although both are served. It is here that the Muslim influence has created the magnificent Mughlai cuisine. This is the most lavish cooking of all. It's said that a good Punjabi cook can produce a different lamb dish for every day of the year, whether it's spit roast, barbecued, baked or skewered. This is also the home of the tandoor, the famous oven that produces Tandoori Chicken or Lamb. The birianis and pilaus of the region are famed throughout India. Here dal is served with nearly everything — not perhaps surprising when you learn they grow over 60 varieties of lentil.

In Bengal many Hindus refer to fish as the 'fruit of the sea' so that as vegetarians they can still eat it, because the seafood of this area is superb. Hilsa is a magnificent creation of delicately spiced fish wrapped in pumpkin leaves for cooking. Rice is consumed with slightly less gusto than in the south, and dal is omnipresent but not with the varieties of the Punjab.

In fact the food of Bengal is generally plainer than elsewhere, but the cooks are inventive and they will resort to flowers and unusual fruits for variety. One of their specialities is a curry of bamboo shoots. In the sweet department they are paramount, and Bengal confections are renowned in famous sweets like Ras Gullas, Ras Malai and Gulab Jamons.

The cuisine of the western region seems to be an amalgam of many different areas, possibly because of the presence of many small but influential groups like the Parsees, Goans, Gudjeratis and Pathans. The Gudjeratis specialise in vegetarian dishes and the Goans, with the Portugese influence emerging, contribute dishes like Pork Vindaloo. The cooks in Bombay tend to add sweetness to many unlikely things like lentils and vegetables.

In the course of researching for this opus I have peered into a lot of the old cookery books of Imperial India. I have been mystified by many things, including the variety of different spellings which I suppose is the inevitable result of transliteration — yet they all claim to be Hindi.

For instance, sultanas appeared in one glossary as 'kishmish', only to surface in another as 'munuckha'; spinach was 'sag' or 'palak'; the humble tomato became 'belatee bygun' or 'tamatar'. So I have tried to stick to English where I can. I have been baffled by bazaar weights and measures with enchanting names like pusseree, hooghly seer, chittacks, pows and maunds. So I'm not using those. I'll use teaspoons and metrics instead.

Many of the publications of the period contain household hints and I've learnt how to 'vanish' fleas and bugs, what to do with old chamois leather gloves, and how to deal with scorpion stings, as well as having the benefit of innumerable experts 'observations on the kitchen and its requirements'. From the latter I offer a suggestion of no little importance, viz, cats, dogs and sweepers as a rule have no business in the kitchen. The sweeper, or, as he is elsewhere called, 'the knight of the broom', should be admitted either before the operations of the day have commenced, or after their termination. Then comes the warning that if you don't watch out 'not only the knight, but his wife also will indulge their fingers in many a savoury pie': sage advice from *The Indian Cookery Book* by 'Thirty-five Years a Resident', published in 1917 by Thacker, Spink and Co. of Calcutta.

PRESENTATION

In some of the remoter fastnesses of the world where, when gentlemen gather to dine, it is common to belch in appreciation of the food, it is better not to inquire after the health of the lady, or ladies, of the house — unless it is one of 'those' houses. The opposite is also true. Borborygmi and belching don't go down (or up) too well in Bognor or Boston, but polite inquiries after the health of the ladies are well thought of. As a masochist might have said, 'other folks, other strokes'.

So please don't eat Indian food with a knife and fork. Use a fork and spoon, or, better still, use the fingers of your right hand. The atavistic remnants of elementary rules of hygiene decree the left hand unclean. Various interpretations of etiquette surround fingering. The northern Indian is very particular about using only the tips of his fingers, whereas in the south it's considered quite acceptable to plunge in up to the knuckles, or even immerse the whole hand. But dainty or bold, it's a very fulfilling way of eating. After getting used to it, one enthusiast declared that to eat with utensils is like taking a bath with your mackintosh on. However, it requires practice, so settle for a compromise. Tear off a piece of chapati or naan or paratha and use it as a scoop, and combine this technique with the fork and spoon. When you become an addicted adept, you'll probably dispense with the utensils.

When food is presented in India it normally appears on a thali, a circular tray of silver, brass or stainless steel. One or two small bowls called katoris contain the more liquid dishes, with the rice, chapatis and other dry foods placed directly on the tray. In the south of India, banana leaves are a delightful substitute for the tray and the katoris are little clay pots which are discarded after the meal. Not all of us, alas, have easy access to banana leaves, so we'll have to make do with Wedgewood.

The rice is served first in the manner of the thali, with the other delights arranged around. It's really wrong to mix everything up together, unless you are the sort of person who enjoys churning up your *filet mignon* with the *pommes gratin dauphinois* and *choufleur à la niçoise* — because that's what it amounts to.

Every dish has a character to be savoured in its own right, each curry its own mystical blend of spices best appreciated against the blander background of rice. Soups are sometimes served, but rarely at the beginning of a meal — but then if you want to, why not? Crisp pappadums, chutneys and pickles complement and cosset the curries. Unleash your imagination in decoration of both the table and the food. Serve samosa on nasturtium or other leaves, for instance, with the blossoms framing the crisp golden pastry. Scoop out melon balls and use the shell as containers for raitas. You probably won't get into the silver and gold leaf with which the princely pulaos of the Punjab are traditionally gilded, but remember at least the principle.

People always sit in armchairs at dinner all over India.
— Lady Canning, c. 1856

UTENSILS AND METHODS

You can festoon your kitchen with seekhs, sil-bathas, chimtaas, or chamchaas; these look exotic and sound impressive — their names are useful words to drop in one-upmanship situations — but you don't need them. Any reasonably equipped kitchen will have everything you require. Modern processors are marvellous and indispensable for anyone with a serious interest in cooking. They chop, blend, crush and liquefy, simplifying the whole business of food preparation. If you don't have one, however, a mincer or a pestle and mortar are fine. After all, we were at it long before machinery came along.

A chinese wok is the only utensil you may not have. It's very useful, but not indispensable. An iron frying-pan is also very handy. A word about the care of this. Never wash your frying-pan, or use a metal knife or sponge in it. Clean it with heat and salt, using paper towels to wipe with. If you buy a new frying-pan, it's best to prepare it by putting it on a high heat to melt any greasy protective coverings. Wipe it clean with paper, then cover the bottom generously with oil or lard, and heat. Wipe off the excess after pouring away the bulk of the fat, and you're in business.

Spices and metals don't co-exist well, so as far as possible use stainless steel or enamelware, and wooden spoons.

When frying seeds, cover the pan to avoid an attack of little spitting explosions. If adding liquid to frying spices, first remove the pan from the heat, then pour in the liquid from the edge so that you don't get spattered. Many whole spices, incidentally, are more pungent than their powdered equivalents.

If you cook a curry and intend to freeze it, use about half the stipulated masala mixture, as freezing intensifies flavours.

When adding yoghurt to a dish, beat or whip it a little before using it.

KITCHEN METRICS

Dry and Liquid Measures
1 teaspoon (t) = 5 g or 5 ml
1 tablespoon (T) = 15 g or 15 ml = ½ oz
1 metric cup (c) = 250 g or 250 ml = cup approx $\frac{1}{10}$ larger than std 8 oz cup
1 kilogram (kg) = 1000 g = 2 lb 4 oz
1 litre (l) = 1000 ml = 1¾ pints approx

Oven Temperatures	Degrees Celsius	Degrees Fahrenheit	Gas Mark
Very slow	110	220	¼
Cool/slow	140	280	1
Moderate/medium	160	330	3
Fairly hot	200	400	6
Hot	230	450	8
Very hot	240	480	9

A market in Kerala

Ingredients

1. BASIC INGREDIENTS

Agar agar
A gelatinous substance derived from seaweed. It is marketed in sticks, blocks, in strands like masses of fine hair, and powdered. It is far more effective than gelatine as a setting agent, for it is capable of taking up to 200 times its volume of liquid to make a jelly and will produce a dish that never flops.

Chillies
Take care. I've inadvertently rubbed my eyes after preparing chillies. Very painful! It's best to wear rubber gloves. To prepare chillies, begin by rinsing them in cold water. (Hot water will unleash fumes which could irritate your nose and eyes.) Pull out the stem of each chilli under cold running water, then, if the recipe calls for it, seed the chillies by breaking them in half and brushing out the seeds with your fingers. The seeds, which are the hottest part, are sometimes left in by Indian cooks. Dried chillies give flavour and heat, but are not as volatile on the skin — still exercise care, though.

Coconut milk
There are easier ways to get coconut milk than by buying a coconut. Try the variety of canned brands on the market. The milk should smell fresh and sweet, be white and not grey in colour. You can also buy concentrated blocks of coconut cream, containing instructions on how to use it.

Coconut milk can also be obtained from desiccated coconut. There are two stages. The first stage produces thick milk the second thin. Use a mixture of the two unless a recipe specifies one or the other.

Stage 1 Use **2 c desiccated coconut** and **2½ c hot water.** Pour the hot water over the coconut and allow it to cool, then knead it a little and pour it through muslin, squeezing out as much liquid as possible. This is the thick milk. You'll get about 1½ c.

Stage 2 Using the **same coconut** again and **2½ c water,** repeat the process. This will yield a little more, because the desiccated coconut will not absorb as much liquid as in stage 1.

Cream cheese or panir
This is not difficult to make:

Boil **2½ c milk** (or more), occasionally stirring to prevent a skin forming. When the milk starts rising in the pan stir in **lemon juice** — about **1 T to each 2½ c of milk.** Remove from the heat and let it stand for 5 minutes or so. Curds will have formed. Strain through muslin and let it dangle for 30 minutes, then tightly squeeze out the moisture. Weigh it down and leave in a cool place to make it firm.

Dhal or lentils

The literal translation of dhal, dal or dall, is split lentils. It has come to mean any leguminous vegetable seed like peas or beans as well as lentils. There are a vast number of these split seeds, some peeled, some husked, some not. This is a list of the ones most frequently encountered. With the emergence of health-food shops they aren't too difficult to get.

Channa dhal: Bengal split peas, skinned. An ochre colour.
Lobia: Black-eyed beans.
Malka masoor: whole green lentils, sometimes brown.
Massor dhal: red split lentils, skinned.
Matar ki dhal: split peas, yellow and green.
Moong (mung) dhal: green chickpeas, split and husked. Inside the green coat it is a pale yellow.
Rajma: red kidney beans.
Toor dhal: red chickpeas.
Urhad dhal: black chickpeas, husked. A greyish-white colour inside. When soaked and ground and left for an hour or so, it has the property of fermentation, making the mixtures in which it's used light and spongy.

Garlic (Lasan)

Vital in many cuisines including the Indian, although banned by Kashmiri Brahmins for its effect on the baser passions, garlic is prized not only for its flavour, but also for its health-giving and magical properties. There are many different types. I have specified finely chopped amounts in teaspoons, $\frac{1}{2}$ or 1 or whatever. It achieves a certain uniformity. Crush the pieces to release the volatile oils after measuring and before cooking. If they are going in the blender, of course, you don't have to bother.

Ghee

This is virtually clarified butter. You can buy it or make it:

Take say, **500 g butter,** cut it into quarters and slowly melt it in a large saucepan, stirring it to prevent browning, then bring it to the boil. When the surface is covered with a white foam, stir gently and reduce the heat to the lowest possible point, and simmer for about 45 minutes, until the milk solids on the bottom are golden brown, and the butter covering it is transparent. Now strain the liquid into a bowl through a fine, linen-lined sieve, or 4 layers of damp cheesecloth. If there are any solids in the ghee, strain again to prevent it from becoming rancid at a later date. Pour it into a crock, cover tightly and store in the refrigerator. This ghee will solidify when chilled. In recipes that require liquid ghee, melt it, but don't brown it. It will keep at room temperature for 2–3 months.

Ginger

Again I specify amounts chopped and measured in teaspoons. Before chopping or grating, scrape off the skin with a sharp knife.

Onions

Despite isolated religious objections, onions are an essential in almost every curry. Asian onions are reddish purple, but you can use brown or white onions instead. They vary considerably in size, and since I specify small, medium or large onions in the recipes, it might be just as well to define what is meant. A small onion is around 60 g, a medium is about 125 g and a large one 250 g or more.

Weigh a few to get the idea, but total accuracy isn't essential, so don't bother weighing them every time you create a curry.

With the emergence of new food-processing machines, nobody need weep over the onions any more, except possibly when cutting onion rings, which are sometimes called for. Incidentally, the best way to cut rings is to take a small slice off the peeled onion, and use the flat facet as a base. Much easier than the confusing trick of balancing the sphere! As for the tears, I've been told many methods — from cutting near a running tap to holding a toothpick or small teaspoon between the teeth. The best method is to enlist someone else!

Rose essence
A common ingredient in drinks and Indian sweets, this fragrant essence can be purchased at the chemist. A diluted version, rose water, is also usually available.

Yoghurt
You can easily make your own.

Mix **1 T cultured yoghurt** with **600 ml boiled lukewarm milk.** Keep in a warm place for about 4 hours. When it has set, it's ready. Commercial yoghurt made from milk solids or skimmed milk, and chemically soured, won't do as a starter, but once you have established your own, you're off and running. Save back a tablespoon from each batch to make the next one.

The above are most of the basic ingredients. Other major ones will be found in their relevant sections.

2. SPICES AND MASALAS

The fascination of Indian cooking lies in the blending of the spices, and these magical blends are called masalas. There is only one inflexible rule: no curry powders. There are certain requirements for certain dishes, but the variations are almost infinite, and even the best Indian cooks will discuss endlessly the structures of their masalas.

The three functions of spices in Indian cooking over the centuries have become separated, so that the medical and preservative qualities have become secondary to the concern with flavour, although it's nice to know it's healthy. Some of the old ideas are still practised, their origins half forgotten. Legumes, for instance, will often be cooked with mint, dill, ginger or asafoetida, which are all reputed to counteract flatulence. And legend still has it that highly-spiced food stimulates the liver, which is apt to become sluggish in the tropics.

A few obvious principles emerge with practise, but they're really common sense. Certain spices are too strong for delicate dishes, so they are used sparingly. Turmeric, for instance, is rarely used in dry vegetable dishes that require a short cooking time because it needs a sauce to mellow it. Similarly, a garam masala is seldom used with fish or vegetables because its pungency would overwhelm the delicate taste of the main ingredients.

In other dishes the spices are used not only for flavour, but for texture. The poppy seeds, ground cinnamon sticks, cardamoms and cloves in a korma, for instance, are as necessary for their texture as for their flavour.

In certain pilaus the fragrance of saffron is all important, while in other dishes the spices are used to give the right colour. Invariably it's a question of balance, related to the major requirement of the dish.

One or two other generalisations emerge. Northern Indian cooks tend to use more dry spices than their southern counterparts, pounding them into a powder rather than grinding them with a liquid to make a paste. Groups of ladies, in fact, who are professional spice pounders wander round the houses in the north, setting up their cumbersome apparatus to pound a month's supply of spices for you.

In the south they prefer fresh or green spices which cannot be stored. They grind these up with lime juice, coconut cream or vinegar to make wet masalas which vary in consistency according to the amount of liquid used. Wet masalas blend more easily into a sauce, and the great rice eaters of the south have more liquid dishes in their repertoire than the northern Indians who have an immense range of dishes where the sauce is reduced to a bare minimum.

A final observation is that it's not *what* spices are used, so much as *how* they are used that counts. They should never have a raw taste, never catch in the throat or intrude to the extent that the essential character of the dish is overwhelmed. Bear in mind that all cookery books are only guides really, and of all the culinary disciplines, Indian cooking allows the greatest latitude for invention, so in the use of spices you can express your personality, your talent and your culinary vision.

Spices – Barks, Berries, Leaves and Seeds
(Hindustani names in brackets)

Ajowan (Ajwain)
Comes from the same family as parsley and cumin, but the flavour is that of thyme. Used in lentil dishes. Ajowan water is used as a carminative.

Aniseed (Souf)
The leaves of anise can be used for garnishing, giving a slightly sweetish flavour. The seeds are very powerful and should be used with discretion.

Asafoetida (Hing)
A resin obtained from the roots of a plant in the fennel, parsley and carrot family, this ingredient's prime purpose is again to flatten flatulence. It doesn't smell very pleasant on its own, but used in minute quantities it imparts a distinctive flavour that is highly thought of.

Bay leaves (Tejpattar)
Used in Northern Indian dishes and vindaloos.

Cardamom (Eelachie)
The most expensive spice after saffron, cardamom is the seed pods of a member of the ginger family. There are two varieties. One is large and darkish, the other smaller and pale green. The smaller variety is sometimes bleached in processing. It's easier to get the small ones and they can perfectly well be used in place of the large ones.

Chillies (Lal Mirchi)
Several varieties are available. As a rule the smaller the hotter, and the seeds are the hottest parts of all. There are green and red chillies. Goan and Kashmiri chillies are less pungent, and the capsicum is a much milder variety of the family. Chilli powder is made from ground chillies.

Cinnamon (Darchini)
Cinnamon has a relative called cassia, which is very similar, but not as subtle. In many countries they are confused. It is better to use true cinnamon. Buy cinnamon sticks or quills rather than the ground spice which dissipates its flavour quickly. Cinnamon quills have a thin palish bark, sun dried to form quills packed inside each other. Cassia bark is thicker.

Cloves (Laung)
The clove tree is an evergreen, native to South-East Asia. It grows to about 10 m and has scarlet flowers. The cloves are the dried flower buds. They very considerably in size, appearance and pungency, depending on their age and origin. They should be full and not shrivelled. The clove is a powerful antiseptic, but in cooking must be used with discretion as it can be overpowering.

Coriander (Dhania)
A lacy-leaved annual, also called cilantro and chinese parsley. Both the seeds and the leaves are used. The seeds are used dried and ground, and emit a warm aroma with a hint of sage and lemon peel. Coriander is used in Indian food much as parsley is in European cooking. You can buy it fresh in bunches, complete with roots. To store it, leave on the roots, wrap it tightly in a plastic bag to eliminate as much air as possible, and place it in the refrigerator. It will keep for up to a week or more. It is also very easy to grow.

Cummin (Sufaid Zeera)
An extremely aromatic seed, from a small annual herb of the parsley family. Looks like a caraway seed, but the flavour is totally different. Like coriander, an essential ingredient in Indian cooking.

Cummin, black (Kala Zeera)
This is not a true cummin, and it has a different aroma and a peppery flavour. An essential ingredient in Panch Phora (a combination of five different aromatic seeds).

Curry leaves (Kitha neem, Katnim)
Small shiny leaves of a tree native to Asia. Keep their flavour well when dried. Used fresh where the tree is abundant. They can be fried in the preparation of a curry or pulverised in a blender and made into a powder. As important to curries as bay leaves are to a stew — but don't try and substitute one for the other.

Fennel seeds (Sonf)
The leaves of this common plant are more widely used than the seeds, which have a slight, anise flavour, but not as sweet. It's sometimes called sweet cummin.

Fenugreek (Methi)
Both the leaves and the seeds of this leguminous plant are used. It is an annual, rather like clover with a brilliant colour. Indians use it fresh in salads but it is rather bitter. The small, squarish, flat seeds are sandy brown, but must be used with caution because of the bitterness. Good in fish curries, when they are fried gently at the start. Can be used in powder form. It is fairly easy to grow.

Ginger (Adrak)
The pungent root of a sweet plant which resembles an iris. It has a light brown skin and the flesh is firm and pungent. Powdered ginger cannot be substituted, for the flavour is quite different.

Kewra water
An essence derived from the screw pine. Very strong in its natural form. Available from shops that specialise in Indian ingredients.

Mace (Javatri)
The husk of nutmeg, but more delicate. Sometimes used in meat and fish curries.

Mint (Podina)
The common round-leaved mint is the most widely used of many varieties. Used in many different dishes — e.g. chutneys, koftas and drinks.

Mustard, black (Rai, Kimcea)
A more pungent seed than the larger yellow variety. An oil is extracted which is widely used in Bengal and Kashmir, often in pickles.

Nutmeg (Jaiphal)
Occasionally used in curries, more often in confections. Must be used sparingly.

Pepper, black (Kali Mrich)
The berries of a tropical vine. They grow in strings, first green, then bright red. Black peppercorns are picked green and then dried in the sun.

Poppy seeds (Khas Khas)

There are black and white poppy seeds. The white seeds are used for thickening gravies, since flours and other starches are never used. Black poppy seeds can't be used as they have a different flavour. If you can't get the white seeds, substitute ground almonds.

Saffron (Kesar)

The most expensive spice in the world. It comes from the orange-coloured stigmas of a mauve-coloured crocus, which have to be hand picked, and it requires over 200,000 of them to make 500 grams. Do not confuse it with turmeric, often sold as Indian saffron. Cheap saffron will probably be safflower or bastard saffron. It looks similar but has no fragrance.

Sesame Seed (Til ka tel)

The seed of an aromatic annual. The tiny white toasted seeds have an almond-like flavour. Sesame-seed oil is a sweetish oil used in some parts of India.

Tamarind (Imli)

The fruit or pod of a handsome tropical tree, which grows to a great height and age. It is believed that the acid pulp is effective against fevers. It is sold dried in packets with the instructions inside.

Tulsi (Tulsi, Tookmeria)

Tiny black seeds of a plant of the basil family. They look like poppy seeds until they are soaked in water, when they develop a transparent slippery coating. They are used in cold drinks, as they are said to cool the body — a valuable property in hot climates.

Turmeric (Haldi)

The fleshy root of a brilliant tropical plant of the ginger family. Can have a slightly bitter and resinous flavour, but it is widely used. Gives colour, but must not be confused with true saffron.

CURRY-EATING SPECIALIST FINED £5

A stranger in an Indian restaurant in Southend tried to demonstrate to Mr Arthur Flint how he should eat his curried chicken and rice. Mr Flint demonstrated his displeasure by pushing the curry in his face. In return, Mr Flint received a blow on the head with a chair.
— Evening Standard, London, 1967

Masalas

These are some basic mixtures. The garam masalas are the ones you'll use most.

It makes no difference what size measuring spoons you use, so long as you are consistent. Don't change spoons in mid-masala, and keep your measures level. The cup is a standard 250 ml measuring cup. I have included several garam masalas, to show the differences. In time you'll create your own. All these will keep for 4-6 months in airtight containers. Keep the proportions, but you can vary the amounts made.

Garam Masala 1

1½ T black cummin seed
1½ T white cummin seed
½ c coriander seeds
4 T cardamom seeds
6 T cloves

¾ c black peppercorns
2 T grated nutmeg
4 T crumbled cinnamon stick
3 bay leaves

Roast all the ingredients at 160°C for about 10-15 mins, then grind together to a fine powder and press through a fine seive. Keep in airtight containers.

Garam Masala 2

1 c cummin seed
6 T fennel
6 T cardamoms

1½ T cloves
1½ T cinnamon
1 T mace

Lightly roast all ingredients. Note that different roasting times are needed for different ingredients. The cloves and cinnamon take about 7 min, the cardamoms and nutmeg about 4-5 min, and the cummin seeds and fennel about 3 min. You can roast them on silver foil under the grill — adding as you go. After roasting, grind together to a fine powder and keep in an airtight container.

Garam Masala 3

2 T cardamom
1 T cummin, black
2 T cinnamon

1 t cloves
1 t mace
1 t nutmeg

Roast and grind as before.
If you add **1 T black peppercorns** to this one, you have a Kashmir Masala.

Sambhar Masala 1

This is a Southern India masala, sometimes called Madras Rasam.

2 T cummin seeds
2 T coriander seeds
2 T black beans

½ T fenugreek seed
1 T black peppercorns

Fry ingredients separately in a heavy-bottomed pan for a few minutes. Grind to a fine powder and store in airtight containers.

Sambhar Masala 2

This is a hotter masala with a quite different flavour.

6 T coriander seeds
1 T fenugreek seeds
1 T cummin seeds
1 T mustard seeds
20 black peppercorns
10 curry leaves

2 t turmeric powder
½ t asafoetida powder
1½ T chillies
2 T dried black beans,
     chickpeas and lentils mixed

In a heavy-bottomed pan fry separately all the ingredients except the turmeric and asafoetida. Add the latter, then grind all to a fine powder and store in an airtight container.

Green Masala Paste

This gets the colour from the use of fresh coriander leaves and mint.

1 t fenugreek seeds
1 T chopped garlic
2 T chopped fresh ginger
1 c packed fresh mint leaves
1 c packed fresh coriander leaves
½ c vinegar

3 t salt
2 t ground turmeric
½ t ground cloves
1 t ground cardamom
1 c vegetable oil

Soak fenugreek seeds overnight. They will swell up. Measure 1 t soaked seeds and blend, on high speed, with coriander and mint leaves, garlic, ginger and vinegar. Blend until fine and smooth. Mix in rest of ingredients. Heat oil until very hot, add mixture, bring to boil and turn off the heat. Cool and bottle in airtight container. Oil should cover the mixture totally to ensure an airtight seal. If it doesn't, heat some more oil and add it to the container.

Madras Curry Paste

2 c ground coriander
1 c ground cummin
2 T each ground black pepper,
    black mustard, chilli powder,
    turmeric and salt

4 T each crushed garlic and
    fresh ginger, finely chopped
Vinegar for mixing
1½ c ghee

Combine ground spices and salt in bowl. Add garlic and ginger to vinegar and mix to a smooth, thick purée. Heat ghee until very hot. Stir in spice mixture and reduce heat. Keep stirring constantly until spices are cooked and oil starts to separate from mixture. Cool and bottle.

Use about 1 T of this paste for each 500 g meat, fish or poultry, substituting it for the garlic, ginger and spices in a recipe.

Tanduri Mix

2 t turmeric	**½ t ground cardamom**
1 t paprika	**⅛ t saffron**
1 t chilli	**½ t garlic powder**
1 t garam masala	

Mix thoroughly and keep in a tightly-capped bottle or jar.

Vindalu Paste

This is for the lovers of the piquant vindalu, and can be used with beef, pork, duck or chicken. The following paste is for 1 kg of meat.

⅔ c ghee or mustard oil	**12 black peppercorns**
1 T ground ginger	**4 cloves**
1 T garlic	**5 cardamoms**
8 red dried chillies	**4 x 2.5 cm sticks cinnamon**
2 T coriander seeds	**1 t salt**
1 T cummin seeds	**Vinegar to mix**
3-4 bay leaves	

Grind ingredients and combine in a bowl with salt and vinegar to make a thick purée. Heat oil or ghee in a saucepan, and when very hot add purée. Reduce heat and stir constantly until the spices are cooked and the oil separates from them. Cool and store in airtight container. When used in a vindaloo add more vinegar for the marinade, and use in place of masala in recipe.
Note: When tightly bottled with plenty of oil, this keeps for a good while, and is suitable for despatch round the Cape.

Panch Phora

Panch means five, and this is a combination of five spices. Panch Phora needn't be ground and more often than not it isn't. I've unearthed three varieties, so take your pick.

Combine the various ingredients listed for each mixture.
Store in airtight containers. Shake before using.

1. **Equal parts of mustard seed, aniseed, cummin, cassia leaves and red chillies.**
2. **Equal parts of cummin, fenugreek, aniseed, mustard seed and black cummin.**
3. **Two parts black mustard seed, cummin seed, black cummin seed, one part each fenugreek seed and fennel seed.**

Breads

Until the arrival of the British in India, bread made with yeast was virtually unknown. The vast majority of people then, as now, ate unleavened breads. These breads, made mostly from whole grains, are delicious and nutritious.

In Northern and Central India, wheat is the most popular grain, but flours made from maize, lentils, rice, and millet are also utilised. A special wholewheat flour called atta is the best, but a fine ground wholewheat flour is a good substitute where atta is not available.

The humble chapati is the daily bread of most Indians and quite a few elephants. But there are many breads, ranging from the gossamer-thin Rumali Roti, flung in the air to achieve lightness, right through to cartwheel size chapatis for elephants.

The single most important step in breadmaking is the preparation of the dough. On damp days you will find that you may need a little more flour, for instance. If your dough sticks to your hands, or the bowl, after combining all the ingredients, keep kneading and add a little more flour until the dough comes away from the bowl clean. Always knead until the dough is soft and pliable. When leaving dough to stand, always cover it with a damp cloth.

And remember, the more you knead, the better you get!

Chapatis

675 g wholemeal flour   **4 T plain flour**
Pinch salt   **Water to mix**

Turn wholemeal flour and salt into a bowl and slowly mix in enough water to make a pliable dough. Leave for 30 minutes. Knead again. (One of the secrets of light chapatis is to fold in as much air as you can when kneading.) Pull off pieces about the size of ping-pong balls, roll into spheres, dip in plain flour and flatten them out into circles with a rolling pin.

Heat an iron griddle or flat iron frying-pan until very hot. Drop in the flat chapati and cook 15-20 seconds each side, until it starts to puff up slightly and brown spots appear. Press lightly with a cloth and the chapati will puff up perfectly. I then pass it quickly over a naked flame to really complete the puffing-up process.

Delicious with wet curries, and a very useful eating instrument.

I am this world and I eat this world. Who knows this. Knows.
— Upanishads, 7th Century BC

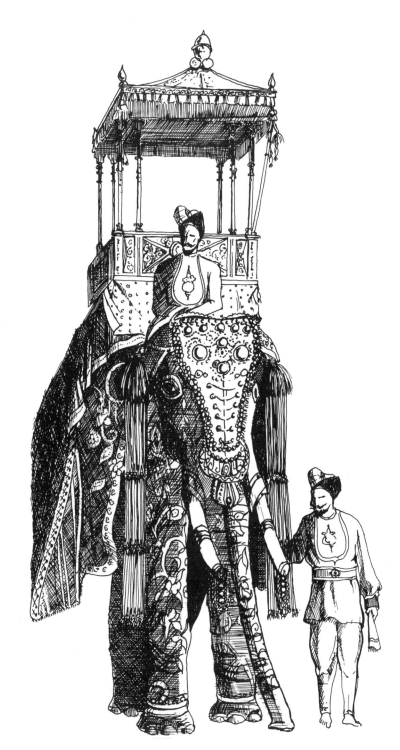

A well dressed elephant

Puris

Use the same dough as given for Chapati (p. 23) but roll out the balls into circles about half the size. Deep-fry one at a time, in about 2.5cm of hot fat. Spoon hot fat over the puri until it puffs and swells. Turn over and continue frying in the same way. When both sides are pale golden brown, drain on absorbent paper.

Buttered Wholewheat Unleavened Bread (Parathas)

2 c wholewheat flour	**½ t salt**
About 1 c water	**Ghee**

Make up the dough as for chapatis. *(See p. 23)* Leave to stand. Have some liquid ghee to hand. Roll out little balls of dough, using a little dry flour. Don't make them too thin. Over each one spread a spoonful of ghee. Fold and spread on more ghee. Repeat this 2 or 3 more times and finally roll out fairly thinly. Grease your griddle or thick-bottomed iron frypan and bake one side of the paratha. Grease the top side of the bread and turn it over to cook the other side. Turn again if necessary. Parathas take longer than chapatis to cook, and you must beware of burning.

Stuffed Parathas

Dough made up as above

Stuffing

2 potatoes	**1 t salt**
1 T ghee	**½ t garam masala**
1 med. onion, finely chopped	**½ t chilli**
1 T finely-chopped fresh coriander	**1 T lemon juice**
1 cm piece chopped ginger	

Boil, peel and mash the potatoes. Fry the onion, coriander and ginger for a few minutes until the onion is soft. To this add the garam masala, chilli powder and salt. Mix with the mashed potatoes and sprinkle with lemon juice. Fry for a couple of minutes and allow to cool. Roll out the paratha (not too thinly), spread on the ghee and place 1 T of the stuffing in the centre. Fold the edges over the stuffing and roll out again as thinly as possible, using a little dry flour. Cook as for parathas.

Flat Baked Bread (Nan)

2 c plain or wholewheat flour	**1 T ghee**
½ t salt	**½ c milk**

Sift flour with salt and rub in the ghee. Gradually mix in the milk and a little water to make a soft dough. Form into flat cakes about 300 mm across and 6 mm thick. Bake in a hot oven until firm and crisp.

Nans are ideal for stuffing. Make a slit in the side and fill with a salad, vegetables or whatever takes your fancy.

Stuffed Puris (Pirhi Puri)

Puri dough *(See p. 25)*
Stuffing

½ c black beans
2½ cm piece finely-chopped ginger
2 cloves crushed garlic
½ t chilli powder
1 T coriander seeds

½ t white cummin seeds
Salt to taste
Lemon juice
Oil for frying

Soak the beans for at least 4 hours. Dry thoroughly and grind up with the spices, salt and lemon juice. Roll out the dough in the usual way and place 1 T of the stuffing in the centre. Roll up and flatten, taking care not to break the puri. Deep fry in the usual way.

These can be served hot or cold.

Semolina Puris (Suji Puri)

3 c wholewheat flour
4 T chickpea flour
2 T semolina

½ t chilli powder
2 T ghee

Mix flour and semolina. Mix in the chilli, salt and ghee. Add enough water to make a stiff dough and knead well. Cover with a damp cloth and leave for an hour. Knead again and cook like Puris.

Cornflour Chapati (Makke ki Roti)

500 g cornflour
2 T ghee

Water

Sift the cornflour into a basin and add enough water to make a pliable dough. Knead for about 15 minutes, then leave uncovered under a damp cloth for 10 minutes or so. Knead again for 10 minutes. Divide up the dough into walnut-sized balls and roll out flat. Cook as for chapatis. Serve hot with ghee.

Hoppers

These Southern Indian pancakes are very popular at breakfast. In the original manner they are so cooked that they have a lacy edge, but we can approximate the method by using an omelette pan which enables us to swirl the batter up the sides to get the same effect.

1 c basmati rice *(See p. 28)*
1 t salt
½ c coconut milk

Pinch of bicarbonate of soda
Ghee

Grind up the rice and mix it with the salt, coconut milk and soda. Leave it overnight. Before using whip up the batter well — this will make the hoppers light. Grease the pan with a little ghee, put it on a medium heat and pour in a little of the batter. The instant you add the batter, swirl the pan so that it runs up the sides. The moment it solidifies in the centre, remove with a fish slice. Store in a warm cloth.

Steamed Lentil and Rice Cakes (Iddlys)

Another Southern Indian breakfast cake. Again, they have a special instrument in India for making these, but an ordinary egg-poacher will do.

½ c urad dhal   **Scant cup rice**
2 t salt

Soak the lentils and rice separately for up to 6 hours. Grind each to a smooth paste, combine and allow to stand overnight. Add the salt and beat slightly. Line the egg-poacher with damp muslin. Fill each depression with the mixture, then cover with another layer of damp muslin. Alternatively, you can just grease the egg receptacles and spoon in the mixture. Either way, cover the pan and steam for 10 minutes on a high heat. Eaten with Sambar or any other soup-like purée (*See* Soups, p. 43) and chutney.

Sarawasti, Goddess of Learning

Rice

Rice, one of mankind's oldest cultivated crops, is Southern India's gift to the world — or so the pundits pronounce. Records going back over 5000 years tell of rice cultivation in India and China, and today over half the world get their calories from rice. There are said to be over 7000 different varieties, and India alone boasts over 1000, with about quarter of all its cultivated land devoted to the production of this ancient cereal grain, known there as chaval.

Rice is revered in India, as it is all over Asia, and it commands a special place in all the religious ceremonies. The symbolic offering of rice is an integral part of religious festivals, and at the exuberant celebration of Pongal in the Southern states, rice is offered to the cattle as a gesture of veneration before the people are served. And don't forget to fill the rice bowl of any holy man you may encounter when wandering abroad. Rice is also a symbol of fertility and the offering of rice at weddings has even survived the long journey to the West, where it is hurled about with gay abandon.

In parts of India, when a little girl starts turning into a big girl she will be initiated into the art of cooking rice. On this special holiday she will cook a dish called Kheer, a sweet rice pudding, for her little brothers. This is the first time she will prepare rice, but by the time she is a woman she will have learned how to cook rice in at least 15 different ways.

The hundreds of different types of rice in the marketplaces of India are classified by district, colour and texture. Even the remotest bazaar will boast at least 6 varieties of this honoured grain. I suspect you could cook rice on every day of the year and never repeat yourself. It can be boiled, steamed and fried in diverse combinations. It can be cooked with lentils, other legumes and vegetables, almonds, pistachio nuts, or used with dried and fresh fruits to create delicate desserts.

Rice can more or less be divided into long, medium and short-grained types. Long-grain rice has grains 4 or 5 times as long as they are wide. These long-grained strains are of the patna type and the finest is reckoned to be basmati, grown in the fields by the sacred rivers which flow down from the Himalayas. The grains separate when cooked, and the rice looks light and fluffy. Admittedly basmati is more expensive than other long-grain rice, but in view of the quality, it isn't really a luxury because each grain swells more than with other varieties, so you'll get the same end amount for a smaller initial quantity. Basmati has a superb, nutty flavour, an elusive savoury fragrance and is magnificient in pilau and biriani.

The medium and short-grained types, plumper than their long-grained relative, are moist and tender when cooked, but tend to cling together. They are preferred for milk and rice sweets.

Brown rice has been hulled, but the light-brown bran has been left on; not very popular in India, but used in certain dishes. Most of the rice we get is scraped and polished in mills, but pounding the rice by hand is still the most common method of many of the villages in India. Hand-pounded rice retains most of the nutrients that are lost in milling, and Mahatma Ghandi was a great protagonist of the pounding.

Yet another type of rice is processed by parboiling. This is rice that has been subjected to steam or water treatment before milling, and it is said to retain more minerals and vitamins because of this process.

TO COOK RICE

Everyone has a different way with rice. Some wash it before cooking, some don't. Some soak it, then wash it, and others won't because they think they'll wash away the valuable nutrients. Any method will do if it's carried out properly.

When cooking rice by the absorption method, professionals who know their pots and the heat, measure the amount of water required by placing their middle finger at right angles to the rice and adding water to the first knuckle, but they can almost do it by looking at the pot! Most of us need more precise measures. After all, what about a well-exercised and over-developed long middle finger? Soggy rice!

The age of the rice and the hardness of the water cause variations in cooking, and only after you have cooked unknown rice a first time do you find out the best way to cook it subsequently.

Absorption method

Here are rough rules for cooking by the absorption method.
1. For short and medium-grain rice, use **1 ½ c water** for the **first cup of rice,** then **1 c water** for each **extra cup of rice.** Whether or not you add **salt** is up to you.
2. For long-grain rice, use **2 c water** for the **first cup** rice then **1 ½ c water** for each **extra cup of rice.**

Stirring occasionally, bring the water and the rice to a slow bubbling boil, then clap on a tight lid, lower the heat and cook for about 20 minutes. Remove from heat, lift lid to let steam escape for a minute or two, then fluff it up with a fork. Transfer your exquisite rice to the serving dish with a slotted metal spoon. (Other utensils will squash the grains.)

Boiling method

Plain boiled rice is made quite simply by stirring **1 ½ c rice** into a pan of **rapidly boiling water,** with or without **salt.** In 10-12 minutes the rice should be ready — firm yet tender. Pour into a colander and drain. The grains should be separated, not mashed together and mushy. Some people add a little oil or butter to the water to achieve this; others initially trickle the rice into the pan so that its water never goes off the boil. You'll hit upon your own trick.

There are many ways in which you can give variety to plain boiled rice. You can add nuts and sultanas, colour the rice with turmeric, and stir in a pinch of Panch Phora. In Southern India they would add some grated coconut along with the nuts and sultanas. You can fry up some onions and stir this into the boiled rice, and seeds like caraway and sesame give an interesting texture. Boiled rice is sometimes returned to the pan with 2 t or so of ghee and some ground cummin.

Most of the pulao, pilau and biriani dishes require that the rice be fried before being cooked by the absorption method. Like the Indian breads, these dishes have relatives all over the world. Their nearest kin, of course, are their Middle-Eastern ancestors, but there are others. In Spain it's the paella, and in Italy, varieties of risotto.

Plain Pilau Rice

1 c long grain rice
Salt to taste

2 c boiling water
1 T ghee

Fry the prepared rice in the ghee for a few minutes, stirring it about well so it doesn't stick to the pan. The grains become transparent and then opaque. When they reach the opaque stage, add the boiling water, and the moment the water starts to boil again after being added to the rice, clap on a tight-fitting lid and cook on a simmering heat until the liquid is absorbed. (About 15-20 minutes.) Each grain should be tender and separate.

This is a basic technique for most pilaus and birianis. The only differences are in the spices and other ingredients.

Savoury Pilau Rice

1 c long grain rice
2 T ghee
4 crushed cloves garlic
6 cloves
½ t chilli powder
1 t garam masala
2 c stock

1 medium onion, chopped
2.5 cm piece ginger, finely chopped
5 cm piece cinnamon stick, broken up
2 cardamom pods
¼ c fresh chopped coriander leaves,
for garnish

Fry half the onion and all the garlic until soft and golden. Add the rest of the dry ingredients and the rice and cook until the rice becomes opaque. Add the boiling stock, bring to the boil, clap on the lid and simmer until the stock is absorbed.

Fry the other half of the onion and sprinkle over the finished dish with the fresh chopped coriander as garnish.

This and other pilaus can be further decorated with almonds, slices of hard-boiled eggs, and small red tomatoes. Invent!

Peas Pilau (Matar Pulao)

Makes as Savoury Pilau Rice, but add **1 c peas** — if fresh, at the beginning of frying, if frozen, at the end.

Cauliflower Pilau (Phulgobi Pilao)

Add about **250 g cauliflower sprigs** to the basic Savoury Pilau Rice recipe. Fry the sprigs first, then add the onions, etc. and proceed.

Mushroom Pilau (Khumbi Pilao)

Make as opposite, adding about **250 g mushrooms** instead of the cauliflower. This time fry the onions and garlic first, then add the mushrooms, peeled, washed and sliced, and proceed.

Pea and Cream Cheese Pilau (Matar Panir Pilao)

1 c long grain rice	5 cloves
¼ c ghee	10 black peppercorns
1 finely chopped large onion	5 cm piece cinnamon
3 or 4 bay leaves	4 crushed cardamoms
1 sliced medium potato	1 t ground cumin
225 g panir, cubed and fried	1 t cumin seeds
1 chopped green capsicum	¼ t turmeric
1½ t salt	1 t garam masala
¼ c peas	4 peeled and sliced tomatoes
¼ t chopped coriander leaves	2 sliced hard-boiled eggs

Prepare rice. Fry half the onion, bay leaves and all the spices with the exception of the turmeric and the garam masala, until they are golden. Then add the turmeric, potato, panir and the capsicum and fry for a further 10 minutes.

Boil the rice in another pan until half cooked. Drain and add to the spice mixture. Add the garam masala and stir it all up gently.

Cover with a close-fitting lid and cook another 5–8 minutes until it's fully cooked. Arrange the hard-boiled eggs and tomato slices on the top together with the chopped coriander. Meanwhile you will have fried the other half of the onion, which will be used to complement the final garnish.

Shrimp and Pea Pilau (Jhinga Matar Pulao)

2.5 cm piece fresh ginger, grated	3 heaped T ghee
8 crushed cloves garlic	1 thinly sliced large onion
½ t ground black pepper	500 g long grain rice
1 T ground coriander	1 c thick coconut milk
1 T ground cummin	1 T lemon juice
1 T desiccated coconut	1 t chilli
5 cm stick cinnamon	1 t turmeric
½ t fennel	3 c boiling water
½ c raw peeled shrimps	3 t salt, or to taste
¼ c peas	

Grind together all the spices except the chilli and turmeric. Prepare shrimps and peas. Fry onion until half cooked. Add the ground seasonings and fry another 2 minutes. Add shrimps and continue frying for 2 minutes. Mix in rice and peas and stirring constantly, fry over a low heat for 4 minutes or so, until the rice goes opaque. Pour on the coconut milk and lemon juice, add the chilli and turmeric and about 3 c of boiling water. Bring pilau to the boil again, then cover and simmer until the rice is tender and the liquid is completely absorbed. Decorate and serve.

Chicken Biriani (Murgha Bryani)

8 chicken drumsticks
½ c oil or ghee
½ c chopped almonds
¼ c chopped cashew nuts
1 large finely-chopped onion

4 or 5 bay leaves
2 c long-grain rice
3½ c warm water
1 t salt or to taste

Chicken Paste

1 t garam masala
1 small chopped onion
2 cloves garlic, crushed
5 cm piece ginger
1 c plain yoghurt
Salt to taste

4 cloves
4 cardamoms
½ t turmeric powder
10 black peppercorns
2.5 cm stick cinnamon
½ t saffron strands

Grind together chicken paste ingredients to make a mixture of a smooth consistency. Rub this thoroughly over the chicken pieces. Leave for at least 30 minutes. Heat ghee or oil in frying pan and fry almonds and cashews. Drain and keep for garnish. Fry onion until golden and put aside half for garnish.

Crumble bay leaves and add all the spices except the saffron to the onion remaining in the pan. Add the chicken and, shaking it together, cook well for 20 minutes. Add the rice and mix in well. Pour on the 3½ c warm water and salt, cover and leave to simmer for 15-2 0 minutes until the rice is cooked.

Meanwhile steep the saffron in a little warm water and pound in a mortar. When the rice is cooked, stir in the saffron. Garnish with the reserved onion and fried nuts, and enjoy.

You can use duck instead of chicken for this dish — equally delicious.

Mutton Biriani (Gosht Bryani)

A FESTIVAL DISH

**1 kg trimmed mutton, cut into
2.5 cm cubes
1 t crushed garlic
4 t ground almonds
6 cloves
Salt to taste**

**1 small onion, chopped
1 t ground ginger
1 t chilli powder
1 t ground cummin
2 T ghee or oil
¼ c yoghurt**

Rice

**2 c water
Salt to taste
4 crushed cardamom pods
1 t cummin seeds
Ghee
1 c rice**

**2.5 cm stick cinnamon
½ t rose essence
⅓ c cream (of pouring consistency)
1 T boiling water
½ t saffron strands**

Garnish

**¼ c split almonds, fried
¼ c sultanas, lightly fried**

**¼ c cashews, chopped and fried
1 large onion, sliced thinly in rings and
fried golden brown**

Blend together all the spices and ground ingredients of the first part of the recipe, adding a little water to facilitate the blending. Heat ghee in a pan and add the ground mixture, then fry, stirring constantly until the oil starts to separate slightly. Wash blender jar with small quantity of water and add this liquid to the pan, stirring until it is absorbed or evaporated. Add the mutton pieces and salt and stir until all the meat is well coated. Lower heat, cover, and simmer for about three-quarters of an hour until the mutton is almost cooked. Beat the yoghurt and add to the gravy in the pan. (It should now be nice and thick.)

Prepare rice and put in another large saucepan with the water, whole spices and rose essence. Bring rapidly to the boil, then lower heat. Add a close-fitting lid and simmer gently for about 15 minutes.

Pound the saffron strands in a mortar with 1 T boiling water, then stir in the cream.

Grease a large casserole and spread over the bottom half the rice. Pour over half the cream and saffron mixture, sprinkle with cummin seeds, then cover with a layer of mutton, going right out to the edges. Cover with the remaining rice, pour over the rest of the cream mixture and sprinkle with the rest of the cummin seeds. Cover tightly with foil, crimping the edges carefully, then put on a lid and bake in a moderately-slow oven (160°C), for 40-45 minutes. Serve in the casserole or turn out carefully on to a serving dish. Garnish, and indulge.

*A few threads of saffron put in the water for canaries occasionally makes
a good stimulant.
— Laws Grocers Manual, 1892*

Boiled Rice and Dhal (Kichadi)

This is traditionally made with brown rice, but it can be made with natural short-grain rice also.

1 c brown or short-grain rice	**2 c cold water**
½ c moong dhal	**3¼ c boiling water**
Salt to taste	**½–1 t turmeric powder**
1 t cummin seeds	**1 T butter or ghee**

Soak the washed rice in the 2 c cold water for about 1 hour, then drain well. Wash but do not soak the dhal. Bring the 3¼ c hot water to the boil again, stir in salt, well-drained rice and dhal. Drop in the turmeric and cummin seeds. Cover the pot and cook over a low heat for about ¾ hour, then check the rice and dhal to see that both are quite soft. (This dish should be soft and mushy rather than soft and fluffy.) If it's not quite cooked, add a spoonful or so of water and cook a few minutes more. When it is cooked, stir in the butter or ghee and let stand for a minute or so before serving. *You can use other legumes if you wish.*

Brown Rice

1 c long-grain rice	**2.5 cm stick cinnamon**
2 medium onions, thinly sliced	**6 cloves**
Ghee	**Salt to taste**
1 T brown sugar	**2 c water**

Fry onions until golden, then set aside some of the rings for garnishing. Caramelise sugar in a saucepan until it starts to go dark brown. Pour on ½ c of the water and stir until the sugar dissolves. Set aside. Add the rice to the onions and fry for 4 minutes. Add the cinnamon, cloves, salt and the rest of the water. Lastly pour in the sugar water, then bring to the boil, cover and lower the heat. Simmer until the rice is tender and the liquid absorbed. Garnish with the fried onion rings.

Other rice dishes are in the Sweets section (commencing p. 96)

. . . and all the water drunk into the rice; which may be a quarter of an hour or less. Stir it often with a wooden spatule or spoon, that it burn not the bottom, but break it not. When it is enough, pour it into a dish and stew it.
— Drink was all the Rage in India, Memoirs of Sgt. Pearman

Terence Cooper

Snacks and Appetisers

A multitude of snacks and appetisers gild the Indian culinary lily, covered by the generic name chat. They are in India what the ubiquitous hamburger or pizza is in the West — but only in terms of popularity. There is no comparison between the mostly infantile culinary range of the strip-lit parlour and the infinite variety of the bazaar.

These Indian titbits range from simple roasted chickpeas and puffed rice to a delicious salty, sweet-sour combination offered in deep-fried chips of pastry, chopped vegetables, herbs and chutney. These delights are called Bhelpuri and are sold on the beaches of Bombay from gaily striped stalls.

Then there's the simple snack called Sev, merely a spiced batter pressed through a mould and deep-fried to emerge like delicate crisp noodles. Or the spicy savoury rejoicing in the name of Ghana Jora-garam, which the street vendors of Lucknow sell from great baskets on their heads as they wander about crooning special songs eulogising the singular virtue of their own particular wares. Some of the snacks are more substantial, like Samosas and Shingaras, or vegetables dipped in spiced batter and deep fried, which are called either Pakora or Bhajia.

Many of these snacks are ideal for cocktail parties, or indeed bibulous orgies — they are probably the most delicious blotting paper of all!

Deep-fried Vegetables in Batter (Pakora or Bhajia)

You can use any vegetables or vegetable you like in this recipe.

Batter

2 c chickpea flour (besan)	¼ t turmeric powder
1 c water	¼ t chilli powder
½ t ground coriander	Salt
½ t ground cummin	Pinch of baking powder
1 clove crushed garlic	Squeeze of lemon juice

To make the batter, put the flour in a basin and gradually add the water. Break up all the lumps and get it to the consistency of a thickish pancake batter. Add all the spices, the salt and baking powder, and mix well. Add a squeeze of lemon juice, adjust the seasoning, cover and put aside.

Slice or chop finely the washed and dried vegetables. Heat 2 c of vegetable oil in a wok or a shallow saucepan. (It will be hot enough when 1 t of batter dropped in the oil floats immediately to the surface.) Coat the vegetables as thinly as possible with the batter, lower into the oil and cook until they are a reddish-gold colour.

Remove with a slotted spoon and let the oil drip off into the pan or wok. Place the vegetables on paper towels to remove any residual oil. Marvellous with a little chutney.

Deep-fried Spiced Meat Patties (Samosa)
Makes about 36 patties

Using spring-roll wrappers
Although I am including the pastry recipe here, it is much quicker and easier to buy frozen spring-roll wrappers for encasing the meat. If you do use these wrappers, take out as many sheets as you need and cut each into 3 equal strips. Put 1 t of the filling on one end of a strip, fold over the pastry to make a triangle, then continue folding diagonally until you get to the end, keeping the pattie perfectly triangular all the way. Moisten the edge with water or beaten egg to seal it. Keep the pastry under a dampish cloth until you begin, as it dries out quickly, becomes very brittle, and splinters as you try to use it. The wrappers you don't need can be popped back in the freezer.

Pastry
1½ c plain flour	1 T ghee or oil
½ t salt	½ c warm water

Sift flour and salt into a bowl, rub in oil or ghee, then add warm water and mix until the ingredients are well combined and the dough leaves the sides of the bowl. Knead for about 10 minutes, until the dough is smooth and elastic. Wrap it in plastic or a damp towel and put aside for 30 minutes while you make the filling.

Filling
1 T oil or ghee	1 clove crushed garlic
2 medium onions, minced	1 cm fresh ginger, grated
1 t ground coriander	1 t ground cummin
½ t turmeric powder	½ t chilli powder
3 t lemon juice	250 g minced beef or mutton
½ t chopped fresh mint	1 t garam masala
Oil for deep frying	Salt

Fry onion, garlic and ginger for 4 minutes. Stir in the coriander, turmeric and chilli, then add the meat and fry, turning constantly, until it changes colour. Add a splash of water and the lemon juice and cook until the liquid is absorbed and the meat done. Add the garam masala and allow the mixture to cool, then stir in the fresh mint and mix well. Salt to taste.

If you are using the spring-roll wrappers, follow the procedure outlined earlier. If you have made the pastry, roll out small circles about 15 cm across and cut in halves. Put 1 t of filling on half of each semicircle, brush the edges with beaten egg or water, fold over the other pastry half as a lid and stick down. Samosas should be triangular.

Heat the oil in a wok or a shallow saucepan and deep-fry the Samosas until they are golden brown. Lift them out with a slotted spoon and drain on paper towels. Again, delicious with chutney or raita.

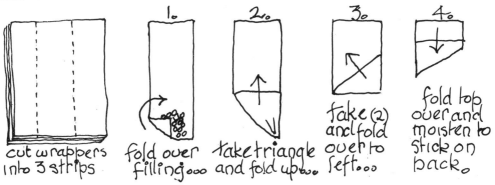

cut wrappers into 3 strips

1. fold over filling...

2. take triangle and fold up...

3. take (2) and fold over to left...

4. fold top over and moisten to stick on back.

Deep-fried Vegetable Patties (Shingara)

These are exactly the same as Samosa but contain a vegetable filling.

Filling

500 g boiled potatoes	**½ c cooked peas**
1 t ground cummin	**½ t chilli powder**
½ t Panch Phora (*See p.22*)	**2 T lemon juice**

Dice the potatoes, mix with cooked peas, lemon juice and spices and proceed as for Samosas.

Deep-fried Peanuts and Rice Flakes with Dhal (Chiura)
Makes about 6 cups

3 T moong dhal	**1 c roasted chickpeas**
1 c raw peanuts	**½ c oil for frying**
1 t black mustard seeds	**2 t ground cummin**
1 t garam masala	**½ t chilli powder**
1 t brown sugar	**Salt to taste**
4 c rice flakes or rice bubbles	

Wash the dhal in a sieve under running water until the water is clear, then soak in a bowl of cold water for at least 20 minutes. Heat ½ c oil in a wok or saucepan and fry the peanuts until they are golden brown, stirring constantly. (Don't let them get too dark.) Remove with slotted spoon and place on paper towel to drain. Toss the roasted chickpeas in the oil, remove quickly and drain. Drain the dhal and pat dry. Fry it in the remaining oil until golden brown, then remove. Add a little more oil to pan if necessary and fry together the mustard seeds and chilli powder until the seeds pop. Lastly add the rice flakes and fry briefly. Remove and place in a bowl, together with the peanuts, chickpeas and dhal. Mix the spices and sugar, add salt to taste, then sprinkle in the bowl and stir thoroughly to distribute the spices evenly. Cool and store in an airtight jar. This will keep for up to 3 weeks in a good airtight container.

Deep-fried Pastry Chips with Chutney (Bhelpuris)
Makes about 80 chips

¼ c rice flour	**Oil for frying**
¼ c plain flour	**6 T chutney**
½ t ground black pepper	**½ c Chiura, prepared as above**
Salt to taste	**one third cup fine chopped fresh**
3–9 T water	**coriander**

Mix flours, salt and pepper in a small bowl. Pour in 3 T water and mix into a dough which can be rolled into a compact ball. If the dough is crumbly, add a little more water, bit by bit, until it's adhesive. Knead it for about 5 minutes until the dough is smooth and elastic, then gather it into a ball, wrap it up in plastic or a dampish towel and set it aside for 30 minutes. Next roll out the dough into a thin sheet and cut into rounds about 5 cm across. (Use a pastry cutter or the rim of a glass.) Place the rounds under a damp cloth while you gather up the scraps, roll them into a ball and cut out more rounds as before.

Heat the oil in a wok or saucepan until a small drop of dough turns brown in a minute, then deep-fry the chips until they are golden brown on both sides, (about a minute or so). Remove with slotted spoon and drain on paper towels.

To serve, arrange on a plate and place 1 t of chutney in the centre of each chip. Sprinkle a teaspoon of Chiura on the top of each, together with a $\frac{1}{2}$ t of the chopped fresh coriander.

The ungarnished chips will keep for 2 or 3 weeks in a good airtight container.

Crisp-fried Chickpeas (Channa Dhal)
Makes about 2 cups

1 c channa dhal or yellow split peas	$\frac{1}{2}$ t garam masala
2 t bicarbonate of soda	Salt to taste
$\frac{1}{2}$ t chilli powder	Oil for frying

Soak the dhal in water with the bicarbonate of soda for about 8 hours or overnight. Drain and wash once or twice to remove any trace of the soda. Spread out on a paper towel and pat dry. Heat the oil and fry the dhal in convenient amounts, then toss it in the mixture of chilli, garam masala and salt. Leave to get cold before munching or storing in an airtight container.

Deep-fried Chickpea Noodles (Sev)

1 c chickpea flour	Salt to taste
1 T oil	Chilli powder
2 T water	Oil for frying
Pinch or two of baking powder	

Put flour in largish bowl, spread the oil over and mix by hand until all the flour feels damp. Now add the water, baking powder and chilli. Mix until you get the consistency of biscuit dough. Heat the frying oil in a wok or saucepan.

There are two ways of making the noodles, either by hand (in which case you break off a chunk of dough and start to roll it out between the palms of your hands to whatever thickness you like), or squeezing the dough through a mouli or potato ricer. Drop the noodles into the hot oil until they turn almost red, then remove with a slotted spoon and drain. You can eat these noodles hot or cold, and they can be stored in an airtight jar for a few days.

Potato Cutlets (Aloo Tikka)

250 g potatoes	3-4 T chickpea flour
2 small minced onions	2 T breadcrumbs
1 t chilli powder	Oil for frying

Boil, peel and mash the potatoes. Mix in the onion, chilli and salt to taste. Make into small oval cutlets. Combine the flour and water to make a smooth batter of coating consistency. Dip the potatoes in the batter and coat lightly with the breadcrumbs. Fry gently until the surface is crisp.

Pea and Potato Patties (Matar Alu Tikka)

450 g potatoes
1 c peas
2 T wholewheat flour
Oil or ghee for frying
2 T grated or desiccated coconut
1 t chilli powder

2 t chopped coriander leaves
½ t turmeric powder
½ t paprika
Juice of ½ lemon
Salt to taste

Boil, peel and mash the potatoes. Boil the peas and mash. Add to these the flour, then fry in the oil or ghee with the spices and salt, stirring this mixture round for a few minutes before removing from the heat. Sprinkle with lemon juice and mix well. Make the potatoes into little walnut-sized balls, flatten and place a little of the pea mixture on each. Fold over a flap of the potato to contain the pea mixture, flatten, coat in coconut and deep fry until golden. Serve hot or cold.

Savoury Batter Drops (Namkin Boondi)

1 c chickpea flour
1 c self-raising flour
1 t chilli powder
1 t garam masala
½ t cummin seeds
Oil for frying

½ t turmeric powder
½ t ajowan seeds, crushed
½ t crushed garlic
Salt to taste
About 1½ c tepid water

Mix the flours in a bowl. Roast the cummin seeds in a pan, shaking until brown, then crush them. Stir these and the ajowan seeds, salt, spices and garlic into the flour mixture, add water and mix into a rather thin batter. Heat the oil or ghee until smoking, then drop small globules of the batter into the oil and fry until golden brown. Remove with slotted spoon and drain.

The best way to get the batter droplets into the oil is to take a slotted spoon, with perforations about the size of a pea, scoop up the batter with it, then tap the spoon so that small fragments drop through the perforations. Adjust the batter to the right consistency. A thicker batter results in more even shapes, but doesn't get as crunchy as the more liquid one. The drops can be stored in an airtight container for some time.

Govern the empire as you would cook a little fish.
— Lao Tze

The following are more usually regarded as breakfast snacks, but they can be eaten at any time. In Southern India breakfast proper often doesn't happen until about 10.30 or so in the morning. Coffee and fruit takes away the early-morning pangs. In the north, breakfast is normally about 7.30 or 8 am.

Savoury Rice and Lentil Pancakes (Dosa)
This makes about eighteen pancakes

1 ½ c uncooked rice
¾ c split black lentils
Salt to taste

1 ½ t sugar
2 t oil or ghee

Soak the rice and lentils for about 6 hours, then drain and grind together into a fine smooth paste. Add the sugar and salt and leave covered overnight.

Heat a heavy-based frying-pan and grease lightly. Pour in enough batter to form a thin pancake, dribble a little ghee round the edge and cook on a moderate heat until crisp and golden underneath. Turn and cook briefly on the other side.

Dosas are often rolled up and filled with a vegetable or meat mixture, then served with lemon juice and paprika sprinkled on top. The following filling is just one of many that could be used.

Filling

500 g potatotes, cut in 2.5 cm cubes
2 T oil or ghee
1 t mustard seeds
3 curry leaves
½ t chilli powder

½ t tumeric
1 large onion, chopped fine
225 g tomatoes
About ½ c water
Salt to taste

Heat oil or ghee in a heavy saucepan or frying-pan until it's almost smoking. Add the mustard seeds and fry until they pop. (Don't forget to cover the pan or you'll be attacked.) Add the curry leaves, salt, turmeric and chilli and stir-fry for about 2 minutes. Add the potatoes and fry for a minute or so. Add the onion, tomatoes and water and simmer for 10 minutes or until the potatoes are soft. If necessary, evaporate any excess moisture to get a dry mixture.

Spiced Rolled Oats (Upma)

2 T ghee
1 t split black lentils (optional)
½ t black mustard seeds
1 medium onion, finely chopped
1 c rolled oats
2 c hot water

Pinch or two of turmeric powder
Salt and pepper to taste
1 t brown sugar or honey
1 chopped tomato
1 lemon
2 T chopped mixed nuts

If you use the lentils, soak them in a tablespoon or so of water for about half an hour, then dry thoroughly and set aside until needed. Melt the ghee in a heavy-bottomed frying-pan, then add the mustard seeds, onion and dhal if used. When the seeds start popping and the onion is browned, stir in the rolled oats. Stir the mixture until it starts to go reddish-coloured then add the water, stirring constantly so that the rolled oats do not form lumps. Now add the turmeric, salt, pepper and sugar or honey. Stir well, add the tomato, squeeze the lemon over and stir again. Top the dish with nuts and cover, letting it stand a minute or two before serving.

Split-pea Flour Cakes in Yoghurt (Pakoories)

½ c split peas
Bicarbonate of soda
Salt to taste(about 1 t)
½ t chilli powder
1 heaped t garam masala

Pinch of baking powder
Ghee or oil for frying
2 t black cummin seeds
1½ c plain yoghurt

Soak the split peas overnight in warm water with a pinch of bicarbonate of soda. Drain off the water and wash to remove the bicarbonate of soda. Grind to a smooth paste, and add the salt, chilli powder and garam masala. Heat the oil in a wok or saucepan, form the mixture into little walnut-sized balls and fry until golden brown. Drain well with slotted spoon. Boil a saucepan of water and add 2 teaspoons of salt. Put the fried Pakoories to soak for 5-6 minutes. Remove with slotted spoon and squeeze slightly to remove any excess water.

Roast cummin seeds under the grill or in a dry frying-pan. Beat the yoghurt and spoon into individual dishes or large serving dish. Add the Pakoories and garnish with the roasted cummin seeds and a sprinkle of salt and garam masala. The Pakoories should be moist and light, therefore don't put them in the yoghurt for more than a few minutes before serving or they will become soggy.

Soups

Soups, as such, don't have the prominence in Indian cuisine that they command in the West.

One of the earliest references to soups in English cooking defines soup as 'a kind of sweet pleasant broth made rich with fruit and vegetables'. The line between soup and broth is hard to define, but the English reference could almost describe many vegetarian curries, and when soup does appear in an Indian meal, it's not primarily as a soup. The idea of soup in Indian cuisine seems to have arrived with the British Raj, who demanded their traditional appetiser before the main meal, but the soups that have emerged are a far bellow from Brown Windsor. However, there's no reason on earth why soup shouldn't be served where-ever and whenever you like.

Yoghurt Soup (Kadhi)

I've heard a theory to the effect that this dish is responsible for the word curry being applied to all Indian food, due, apparently, to the British inability to pronounce 'kadhi'. However, it's an interesting and unusual soup.

8 ½ c water
2 c yoghurt
3 T chickpea flour
Salt to taste
½ t turmeric powder
½ t chilli powder
¼ t ground cummin
¼ t ground coriander

1 t peanut oil
1 dried red chilli without seeds
¼ t mustard seeds
2 cloves crushed garlic
Pinch asafoetida
2 T sugar
¼ c roasted peanuts (optional)

This should be cooked over a low heat to keep the yoghurt from separating, and stirred constantly. Beat together the yoghurt and 1 c water, put in a largish pot and add 7 more cups water. Stir over a low heat for 5 minutes. Mix into a smooth paste the chickpea flour and about ½ c water. Add this to the pot and continue to stir for 15 minutes. You must stir constantly otherwise the flour will form little lumps with the yoghurt, so take care. After the soup has cooked for 20 minutes, add the salt, turmeric, chilli, coriander and cummin. Increase the heat a bit, and cook uncovered for another 20 minutes, stirring often. At the end of the cooking the soup will have reduced its volume by about half and thickened up considerably. Remove from heat and let it stand.

Heat the peanut oil in a small pan. Add mustard seeds, garlic and chilli pepper. When the seeds pop, mix in a pinch of asafoetida and add the whole lot to the soup. Cover for 2 minutes. Add the sugar and stir. Reheat for about 3 or 4 minutes before serving. Often eaten with kichadi.

Pepper Water Soup (Rasam)

These thin soups are digestives. They are sometimes spooned over rice, or taken during or at the end of a meal.

1 T tamarind pulp or instant tamarind	¹/₂ t fennel
1 c hot water	2 t oil
1 t crushed garlic	6 curry leaves
1 t ground cummin	1 t mustard seeds
¹/₂ t ground black pepper	4 c cold water
1 t chilli powder	

Soak tamarind pulp in hot water for 10 minutes. Squeeze and dissolve pulp in the water. Strain and discard the pulp and fibres. Or dissolve instant tamarind in the water. Grind together all the ingredients except the curry leaves and mustard seeds, and put them in a pot with the water and tamarind liquid. Bring to the boil, then simmer for 10 minutes. Meanwhile, fry the curry leaves and mustard seeds in the oil until the seeds pop and the leaves turn brown. Add to the simmering soup. Serve.

Lentil Soup with Coconut (Amti)

1 c split peas	1 T oil
1 t turmeric powder	1 t mustard seeds
Salt to taste	8 curry leaves
8 c water	3 red fresh chillies, seeded and
1 T tamarind pulp or instant tamarind	chopped
1 c hot water	1 clove crushed garlic
1 T brown sugar	2 T desiccated coconut

Soak tamarind pulp in 1 c hot water for 10 minutes. Squeeze and dissolve the pulp. Discard the fibres and pulp by straining. (Or use 1 t instant tamarind dissolved in the hot water.)

Wash dhal well, place in pan with turmeric powder, salt and 8 c water. Bring to boil, reduce heat and cook until the dhal is soft. (About ³/₄–1 hour.) Don't let it get too thick. If it starts to thicken too much, add a little more water. Pour the tamarind water into the mixture and add the sugar.

In a small pan heat the oil and fry the mustard seeds and curry leaves until the leaves go brown and the mustard pops. Add the garlic and fry for another minute. Scrape this mixture and the coconut into the dhal soup and simmer for another 5 minutes. Sprinkle with chopped fresh coriander leaves, if desired.

Vegetable and Lentil Soup (Sambar)

1 c red lentils or split peas	¹/₂ t chilli powder
6 c water	¹/₂ t turmeric powder
1 T tamarind pulp or instant tamarind	Pinch asafoetida
1 c hot water	About 3 c mixed vegetables
1 T oil	2 fresh chillies, seeded and chopped
1 T ground coriander	Salt to taste
2 t ground cummin	1 t mustard seeds
¹/₂ t ground black pepper	1 small onion, finely sliced

Wash dhal or split peas and soak for at least 2 hours. Put in saucepan with the water and cook until soft. Make tamarind liquid as in preceding recipe. Add to dhal.

Heat oil in another pan and fry the ground spices and asafoetida, stirring for 2 minutes. Pour the dhal into this pan, add vegetables and chillies and simmer until the vegetables are done. Fry onions and mustard seeds until the onions are cooked, then add to the soup. Simmer for a minute more and serve.

Pumpkin Soup (Kaddu Soup)

1 medium onion, chopped	Salt to taste
Ghee or oil for frying	1 t ground black pepper
1 large tomato, peeled	Pinch nutmeg
500 g peeled diced pumpkin	Fresh chopped coriander for garnish
1 1/2 c chicken stock	

Fry onion and pumpkin for a few minutes. Puree in blender or push through a sieve. Add stock, nutmeg and seasonings. Bring to boil, then simmer for 15 minutes. Sprinkle with fresh chopped coriander and serve.

Cauliflower Soup (Gobhi Soup)

2 T ghee	2 medium tomatoes, peeled and
1 large onion, chopped	chopped
1 medium carrot, sliced thin	Fresh grated nutmeg
1 small potato, sliced	Salt to taste
1 cauliflower, divided into flowerets	1 t freshly-ground black pepper
Fresh chopped coriander	

Fry onions in ghee for 5 minutes. Add other vegetables and fry a few minutes longer, then pour in chicken stock and simmer until the vegetables are tender. Put through a blender, or mash and push through a fine sieve. Add nutmeg and seasoning, reheat and serve garnished with fresh chopped coriander.

Apple Soup (Seb ka Soup)

2 T ghee	1/2 t garam masala
1 medium onion, chopped	1/2 c hot cream
2 c chicken stock	2 eating apples
1/2 t ground cummin	Juice of 1/2 lemon
1/2 t ground coriander	Fresh chopped coriander

Fry onion in ghee until soft, but not brown. Stir in chicken stock and ground spices. Simmer for a few minutes. Stir in hot cream. Remove from fire and place in blender with one peeled, cored and sliced apple. Blend until smooth, or pass through a fine sieve. Season to taste with salt and pepper. Chill. Peel, core and dice remaining apple and steep in lemon juice. Just before serving, stir in the fresh diced apple and sprinkle lightly with fresh chopped coriander.

Chicken Soup (Murgha Soup)

1 T ghee
2 medium onions, chopped
1 kg chicken, cut in pieces
4 ½ c water

Salt to taste
Ground black pepper to taste
1 t washed rice

Fry onions in ghee. Add chicken pieces and water, and bring to the boil. Cook on lowish heat for about 30 minutes until the water reduces and the soup thickens. Remove from pan and strain. Remove chicken flesh from bones, chop and add to soup with salt, pepper and rice, and cook for another 15 minutes on a low heat. Drop in a few noodles, if so inclined.

Mulligatawny Soup (Gosht Mulgoo Thani)

1 t oil or ghee
1 large onion, chopped
500 g mutton or beef in 2.5 cm cubes
Salt to taste
3 T tomato paste
3 ½ c meat stock
1 large diced carrot
1 t chilli powder
1 T ground coriander seeds

1 t turmeric powder
1 t ground cummin seeds
Pinch grated nutmeg
4 cloves
10 black peppercorns
6 curry leaves
2 cloves crushed garlic
1 t grated ginger
2 sliced lemons (for garnish)

Grind and mix all the masala ingredients together. Add a little water to make a smooth paste. Fry onion in ghee or oil until golden. Add the meat to the pan with the masala paste. Stir it all well and cook for 5 minutes. Add salt, tomato paste and stock. Bring to the boil. Lower heat, cover the pan tightly and simmer for about 30 minutes until the meat is tender. Add the carrot and cook for a further 15 minutes. Remove the meat, mash the vegetables in the soup. Strain and replace the meat. Heat, garnish with the sliced lemons, and serve.

Mulligatawny Soup 2

1 t tamarind water (optional)
Onion rings (raw) for garnish
Approximately 6 c of meat or vegetable
   stock
4 T coriander seeds
2 T cummin seeds

2 T fenugreek seed
1 T mustard seed
2 cloves garlic
12 black peppercorns
6 curry leaves

Boil all in the stock for about half an hour. Strain. Add tamarind water for a really distinctive flavour. Garnish with thinly sliced raw onion rings.

Shellfish and Fish

India has a vast coastline of over 40,000 km, huge rivers and beautiful lakes which boast more than 2000 varieties of fish. Vegetarian Hindus indulge in theological semantics and call all these the fruit of the sea, in order to have their fish and eat it without further soul searching, and the whole riparian population flourishes on fish. Tropical India is a seafood nirvana where fish and shellfish thrive, and the natives roast, steam, bake and boil it, grill, curry and fry it.

From Bombay, naturally enough, comes Bombay Duck, which is not a duck at all but a fish about the size of a herring, very abundant in those waters. It gets its name from its un-fish-like habit of skimming and capering about near the surface of the water like a duck. It is normally cut, cleaned, soaked and cured before it's used. In the raw state it smells vile, but cooked it is delicious. The only way I've eaten it is baked in a high oven until it's very crisp, and then crumbled on to rice. It was delightful — but I must confess that the baking was a bit malodorous.

Incidentally, to prepare a fish without the piscine perfume, I have unearthed a paste which will inhibit it. Combine 2 T of chickpea flour, 1 t turmeric powder and 1 t of salt with about 4 T of water to make a paste. Rub this over the fish and leave it for about 30 minutes, wash it off under the cold water tap, and the perfume will have gone. Let me add that nothing can save tainted fish, although another way of removing an excessively fishy smell is to soak it in a weak vinegar solution, tamarind water, or lemon juice.

Meaty fish are the best for curries, but care must be taken never to overcook them. The same applies to shellfish. In fact it's better to make the dish in stages — starting with the sauce. When that's cooked, and you're almost ready to serve, reheat the sauce and cook the fish in it. Tandoor or baked fish and fish kebabs tend to dry out if not watched carefully. A roasted fish should be generously doused in lemon juice and melted ghee, and it's a good idea to cook it just enough, and then wrap it, while still moist, in aluminium foil or plastic film, thus trapping the dampish air inside. Fish in curry sauces should be well coated in the sauce to keep the flesh succulent and moist.

Some fish dishes can be very complicated and time consuming, but there is a vast array that are quick and simple to make.

SHELLFISH

Cockle Curry

2 c cockles	1 medium onion, finely chopped
1 t cummin seed	1 c water
6 peppercorns	$\frac{1}{2}$ c tamarind water
1 t turmeric powder	1 red chilli
4 cloves garlic	1 $\frac{1}{2}$ t ginger
Ghee	$\frac{1}{2}$ c coconut milk

Wash and scrape cockles well. Grind together cummin seed, peppercorns, turmeric and chilli with ginger and garlic. Fry onion in ghee until golden, add masala paste and fry for another 2 minutes. Add cockles and stir to coat them. Put in about a cupful of water. Cover with close-fitting lid and simmer for about 15 minutes. Next add the tamarind water and coconut milk and cook for about 5 minutes, stirring constantly.

You can cook other shellfish in this manner, adjusting the steaming time. Cockles take rather longer than other shellfish, but they also stand up to a longer cooking time.

Curried Steamed Clams (Teesryo)

3 t ghee or oil	2 c clams
2$\frac{1}{2}$ t scraped and fine chopped ginger	$\frac{1}{2}$ c desiccated coconut
2 large onions, finely sliced and halved	1 freshly-squeezed lemon
Salt to taste	Chopped fresh coriander
2 t ground coriander	Cayenne pepper to taste
1 $\frac{1}{2}$ t turmeric	

Fry ginger for a minute or so, add the onions and fry until golden brown. Stir in salt and ground coriander, fry for about a minute, stir in turmeric and add clams, turning them to ensure they are well covered in the mixture. Cover the pan tightly and steam for about 8 to 10 minutes until the clams open. Scatter over the coconut, sprinkle with chopped coriander, lemon juice and cayenne.

Curried Crab Meat (Kurlleachi Kari)

3 t coriander seed
12 whole black peppercorns
2 crushed cloves garlic
1 ½ t ginger
4 T chopped onion
Salt to taste
1 t ground coriander
1 t ground cummin

½ t turmeric
Ghee or oil for frying
2 c coconut milk
500 g crabmeat (fresh, frozen or
  canned)
Cayenne pepper to taste
Chopped fresh coriander for garnish

Roast and grind coriander seeds and add to coconut milk. Fry peppercorns, garlic and ginger for half a minute. Add onions and fry until golden. Add ground spices and fry, stirring continuously, for 2 or 3 minutes. Add coconut milk, bring to the boil, then simmer for 10 minutes. Add crab meat and cook briskly until this is heated through. Remove from heat, scatter with cayenne and chopped coriander, cover with a tight lid for 5 minutes and let the curry steep.

Bengal Crab Curry (Kakra Kalia)

3 or 4 medium-sized crabs (or 500 g
  crab meat)
3 T ghee or oil
2 medium onions, finely chopped
2 t crushed garlic
2 t fresh grated ginger
3 or 4 bay leaves
2 chillies, seeded and chopped

2 t ground coriander
2 t ground cummin
2 T ground almonds or white poppy
  seeds
Salt to taste
1 c tomato purée
2 c coconut milk
Fresh chopped coriander for garnish

If using fresh crabs, take off the large shells, then remove and discard all the fibrous tissue. Divide each crab into 4 by breaking the body in half and taking off the two large meaty claws.

Fry onion, garlic, bay leaves and chillies until the onions are soft and golden. Add ground coriander, cummin, almonds or poppy seeds, fry a minute longer, then add the coconut milk, tomato purée and salt. Stir well, add the crab pieces or meat, and simmer until the crab is cooked or heated through. If you are using fresh crab, the creatures are done when the shell becomes bright red, and the flesh white and opaque. If using tinned crab meat or cooked crab, adjust the cooking time accordingly. Sprinkle on the fresh coriander as garnish.

You can also use this recipe for crayfish.

Spiced Steamed Mussels (Tisrya Dum Masala)

1 kg mussels	½ t turmeric powder
3 T ghee or oil	3 t ground coriander
2 large onions, finely chopped	Salt to taste
4 crushed cloves garlic	1 c water
3 t fresh grated ginger	1 T fresh chopped coriander
3 fresh chillies, seeded and chopped	Lemon juice

Scrub and beard mussels. Heat ghee or oil in a large pan and fry the onions, garlic and ginger, until the onions are golden. Add chillies, turmeric and coriander and stir in for 3 minutes. Add the salt and water, bring to the boil, then simmer for five minutes. Add the mussels, cover tightly and steam for 8-10 minutes until the shells open. Remove from heat, adjust the salt, squeeze in the lemon juice, thoroughly douse the mussels in the gravy, scatter over the fresh chopped coriander and consume.

Coriander Mussels

32 mussels	1½ t cummin seed
1 t chopped fresh ginger	½ t coriander seed
3 garlic cloves	4 cm fresh green chilli, sliced thinly
¼ c water	1 c minced onion
500 g tinned plum tomatoes	3 T ghee
1 T fresh chopped coriander	Lemon juice

Steam mussels until shells start to open (5-6 minutes). Strain liquid into a bowl and set aside. Discard top of shells and loosen mussels from bottom halves but leave them in these shells. Blend ginger, garlic and water to a thin paste. Heat ghee and fry onion until golden brown. Add garlic and ginger paste. Cook until liquid has evaporated and oil separates from the mixture. Add spices and tomatoes and cook for further 2-3 minutes, stirring constantly. Stir in two thirds of a cup of mussel liquid and sliced chilli pepper over a moderately high heat until mixture is thickened. Add salt and pepper to taste. Stir in fresh coriander. Spoon sauce over each mussel, sprinkle with lemon juice and serve immediately.

And like a lobster boiled, the morn from black to red began to turn.
— Samuel ('Hudibras') Butler, 1612-80

Crayfish or Lobster Curry 1

500 g cooked crayfish or lobster
½ t cummin seeds
10 peppercorns
1 t turmeric powder
4 cloves
4 cardamoms
5 cm piece cinnamon, broken

4 garlic cloves, crushed
1½ t grated ginger
Tamarind water
Ghee or oil
1 medium onion, sliced
Salt to taste

Grind all the masala ingredients, using a little tamarind water to make a paste. Fry the onion until golden, add the masala paste, garlic and ginger. Stir well, and fry for 3 minutes. Add the crayfish, cut up into reasonable pieces, and enough water to make a gravy. Simmer until the cray is heated right through. Salt to taste.

Crayfish or Lobster Curry 2

1 cooked crayfish or lobster (about 750 g)
3 T ghee or oil
2 medium onions, chopped
2 crushed cloves garlic
2 tomatoes, chopped and peeled
1 t ground cummin
1 t ground coriander

2 t turmeric
Pinch chilli powder
2 c milk
1 t garam masala
Salt to taste
Fresh squeezed lemon juice
Fresh chopped coriander

Fry the onions in a largish pan until golden, together with the garlic. Add the chopped tomatoes, cummin, coriander, turmeric, chilli and milk. Cook, uncovered, until the sauce reduces and thickens. (About 45 minutes.) Stir from time to time. Drop in the pieces of crayfish, salt to taste and add the garam masala. Heat through. Squeeze over the lemon juice and serve sprinkled with the chopped coriander.

Crayfish or Lobster with Coconut

1 cooked crayfish or lobster
4 T ghee or oil
1 large onion, chopped
4 crushed cloves garlic
½ t turmeric powder

2 chillies, seeded and chopped
1½ t grated ginger
1 c thick coconut milk
Salt to taste

Fry onions, garlic and ginger until the onion is golden. Add the turmeric, coconut milk and chillies. Simmer for 10 minutes, then add the lobster, cut up into pieces. Heat the lobster or crayfish through. Salt to taste.

You can cook prawns in this way as well.

Prawn and Tomato Curry (Jhinga Tamatar)

500 g peeled prawns
3 medium tomatoes, peeled, seeded and chopped
3 T ghee or oil
2 large onions, chopped
2 crushed cloves garlic
1 1/2 t grated fresh ginger
2 chillies, seeded and chopped

2 T fresh chopped coriander
1 T lemon juice
2 t sambhar masala (*See* p. 20)
1 T brown sugar
1/2 t turmeric powder
Salt
Freshly ground black pepper

Fry tomatoes lightly and set aside. Fry onions until a light golden colour. Grind lemon juice, cummin, chillies and coriander to a smooth paste. Add to the pan with a little water if needed. Put in the prawns, sambhar masala, sugar and turmeric and cook on a moderate heat for 5 minutes. Stir in the tomatoes, salt and pepper to taste. Simmer until the prawns are tender (which shouldn't be much longer). Serve hot.

Sweet and Sour Prawns (Jhinga Patia)

500 g prawns, shelled
1 t salt
1 t turmeric powder
2 t chilli powder, or to taste
6 fresh green chillies, seeded and chopped
1 1/2 t fresh grated ginger

3 t cummin seeds
5 t vegetable oil
3 medium onions, chopped
2 ripe tomatoes, peeled
4 t fresh chopped coriander
1 t brown sugar
1/2 c tamarind water

Sprinkle prawns with salt and chilli powder. Grind together 2 green chillies, garlic, ginger and cummin, adding a little oil if needed. Fry the remaining chillies and set aside. Fry the onions until golden, add the ground spices and cook, stirring, for a few minutes. Add the tomatoes and half the coriander. Add prawns and cook for 10 minutes, pour in tamarind water and brown sugar. Garnish with the remaining fried chillies and chopped coriander.

Great men pride themselves on how to prepare a fish.
— Prosper Montagne

Prawns in Batter (Jhinga Bhajia)

1 c chickpea flour
½ t turmeric powder
½ t garam masala
1 medium onion, finely chopped
1 ½ t grated fresh ginger
A few curry leaves
Salt to taste

½ t chilli powder
1 fresh green chilli, seeded and sliced
½ t bicarbonate of soda
1 T desiccated coconut
250 g peeled prawns
Water

Use enough water to make the flour into a creamy batter. Beat in the rest of the ingredients (except prawns), with salt to taste. Dip the prawns in the batter and deep-fry until a dark golden colour.

Prawn Curry (Jhinga Shorwedaar)

3 T ghee
1 large onion, chopped
1 ½ t fresh grated ginger
2 fresh green chillies, seeded chopped
Salt to taste
1 t sugar
2 T yoghurt
500 g peeled prawns

1 c water
5 cloves
5 cardamoms
6 bay leaves
½ t cummin seeds
1 t turmeric powder
Chilli powder to taste

Fry onion until golden, drain and set aside reserving a few rings for garnish. Grind the spices and chillies together, add to the ghee in the pan, and stir-fry for 2 minutes. Stir in the yoghurt, sugar and salt, cook for 3 or so minutes, then stir in the prawns. Cook for 5 minutes, stirring. Next add the water and simmer for 15 minutes or until the prawns are tender. Serve hot, garnished with the fried onion rings.

Fried Prawn Cakes (Jhinga Kabab)

250 g peeled prawns
1 medium onion, finely chopped
1 ½ t fresh grated ginger
1 ½ t fresh chopped coriander
1 T finely chopped mint
3 T fresh white breadcrumbs
Salt to taste

Fresh ground black pepper
1 egg
3 T fresh squeezed lemon juice
3 T chickpea flour
1 t ground coriander
3 T cold water
3 T ghee

Mince prawns and mix with onions, ginger, fresh coriander, fresh mint and breadcrumbs. Season to taste. Mix well, then add the egg and lemon juice, knead vigorously and leave for 30 minutes. Make a batter with the flour, ground coriander, water and salt. Make prawn mixture into 6 round cakes about 1.5 cm thick. Spread the batter over the cakes thinly, and deep-fry until golden. Squeeze a little lemon juice on each and eat at once.

'Chinese' nets at Cochin Harbour

FISH

Bombay Curry of Eel

1 small onion, sliced
1 crushed clove garlic
Ghee or oil for frying
1 t ground coriander
1 t ground ginger
1 t garam masala

1 t chilli powder
675 g fresh eel
¼ c tomato purée
Lemon juice
Salt to taste

Prepare the eel. Wash it well to remove any slime. Discard the head, or whack it into your fish-stock pot. Chop the eel into 5 cm lengths. Fry the onion and garlic for 2 or 3 minutes, then add the spices and continue frying another 5 minutes, stirring to distribute the spices but prevent them from sticking to the pan. Slowly pour the tomato purée into the pot, and add a little water to make a reasonable amount of gravy. Salt to taste and squeeze in the lemon juice. Now add the eel, stir to cover well with the sauce, and simmer, uncovered, for about 30 minutes. Shake the pan occasionally, rather than stir, to avoid breaking the skins, which will make the fish mushy.

Curried Trout

About 750 g trout
2 large onions, chopped
1 ½ t fresh grated ginger
3 cloves garlic, crushed
2 fresh green chillies, seeded and
  chopped
1 t ground coriander

1 t ground cummin
½ c desiccated coconut
1 T ghee or oil for frying
1 t garam masala
Lemon juice
Salt to taste

Prepare the fish. Blend together one onion and the ginger, garlic, chillies and spices. Add the salt and lemon juice. Fry the other chopped onion until golden then add the ground mixture and stir-fry until the ghee is almost all absorbed. Coat the fish with this paste, wrap it in tinfoil and bake in a slow oven for about 60 minutes.

Fish Sorak

500 g fish
Salt
Freshly ground black pepper
2 red chillies
1 crushed clove garlic
1 t cummin seed

2 t freshly grated ginger
1 t turmeric
1 c coconut milk
1 lemon, sliced
Oil or ghee for frying

Wash and dry the fish, sprinkle with salt and pepper, and fry it gently. Blend together the spices then mix with the coconut milk and put in a pan with the fish and the sliced lemon. Simmer uncovered for 15 minutes.

Fish Croquettes (Machli Tikka)

500 g white fish, filleted and steamed
1 cooked potato, mashed
1 medium onion, chopped
1 t fresh grated ginger
1 clove crushed garlic
1 t fresh chopped coriander

Fresh ground black pepper
2 fresh green chillies, seeded and
  chopped
Salt to taste
2 egg whites, beaten
2 T fresh breadcrumbs

Flake the fish and mix with the mashed potato, spices, onion, garlic, chillies and salt. Make this mixture into about 16 balls. Dip the balls into the beaten egg-white, coat with breadcrumbs and deep-fry until a golden colour. Serve hot with mint or tomato chutney.

Fillets of Flounder with Dill Stuffing (Machli Ki Tikka)

1 kg flounder fillets (or sole, plaice, or
  any other firm, white-fleshed fish)
1½ T lemon juice
About 1½ t salt
1 t fresh ground black pepper
About 5 T ghee or oil
1 clove crushed garlic

2½ t fresh grated ginger
1 T onion, finely chopped
½ t chilli powder
½ t turmeric
Two thirds cup fresh finely chopped
  dill, or 4 t dried dill

Sprinkle washed and dried fish with salt, pepper and lemon juice. Let it steep for about 10 minutes at room temperature. Preheat oven to 180°C (350°F.) Fry garlic, ginger, onions, chilli, turmeric, dill and salt. Stir-fry for about 7 minutes. Test the seasoning. Place even portions of the filling on each fillet and, using a spatula, spread it evenly over the fish. Starting at the narrow end of each piece, roll up the fillets round the filling into a cylinder. Secure with toothpicks. Heat up the oil or ghee in a baking-dish large enough to hold the fillets side by side, place the fish in the pan with the narrow, loose ends of the rolls downward, and cook uncovered (on the top of the stove) for 5 minutes. Transfer the pan to the middle shelf of the pre-heated oven and bake for 12 minutes or so, until the fillets are cooked. (You can test by pressing a finger on to the rolls and seeing if they are firm.) Brown the fish rolls under the grill before dishing and serve with the liquid from the pan poured over them.

Banana-leaf Fish (Patri Ni Machli)

About 750 g firm, white-fleshed fillets,
  or 2 whole white fish of this edible
  weight
2 t salt, or to taste
1 T lemon juice
5 T desiccated coconut
6 fresh green chillies, seeded and
  chopped
6 crushed cloves of garlic

2 t fresh grated ginger
6 T fresh chopped coriander
1 t ground cummin
1 t salt
2 t sugar
4 bay leaves
Banana leaves (or aluminium foil)
2 cinnamon sticks, 5 cm size

Cut the fillets into serving sizes and annoint with lemon juice and salt. If using whole fish, cut the flesh away from the backbone, working from the interior cavities. Cut deep diagonal slits across the flesh and rub in the salt and lemon juice. Grind all the rest of the ingredients to a paste with the exception of the washed and dried banana leaves and the cinnamon sticks. Coat the fish with the paste. Hold the banana leaves over a flame for a minute to soften them, and grease them slightly. Wrap the fish securely in the leaves and tie them up with cotton, or encase in the foil in the usual way. Put the cinnamon sticks in the bottom of a wide deep pan, cover with 5 cm of water and boil. Put the wrapped fish on a rack or plate above the water, cover the pan tightly and steam for about 20 minutes.

Coconut Fish Curry (Machli Moolee)

750-1000 g fish steaks
Lemon juice
Salt
Fresh ground black pepper
6 crushed cloves garlic
6 dried chillies, soaked
3 T desiccated coconut

1 T ground cummin
1 T ground coriander
1 ½ t fresh grated ginger
1 large onion, finely chopped
1 ½ c coconut milk
1 T fresh coriander, finely chopped

Wash and dry fish, rub with lemon juice, salt and black pepper, and set aside. Soak the chillies for about 10 minutes. Roast the coconut in a dry pan until brown, stirring constantly. Fry the onion until golden, then add the ground spices, garlic and ginger. Stir-fry for about 3 minutes. Add the roasted coconut and the coconut milk and simmer for further 3 minutes. Put in the fish and bring to a gentle boil, then turn the heat right down, add the drained chillies and simmer, uncovered, until the fish is cooked. Sprinkle over the fresh chopped coriander when serving.

Sweet and Sour Sauced Fish (Machli Sas)

500 g fish fillets or steaks
Lemon juice
Salt
2 T ghee or oil
1 large onion, finely chopped
2 fresh green chillies, seeded and chopped

1 t crushed garlic
2 T fresh ground black pepper
1 egg
2 t sugar
½ c white vinegar
1 t ground cummin
1 T fresh chopped coriander

Wash and dry the fish, and rub over with the salt and lemon juice. Fry the onions, garlic and chillies until golden. Sprinkle the fish with the pepper. Separately cook this gently in ghee or oil for 5 minutes with a cover over the pan. Turn the fish, sprinkle the other side with pepper and cook for 5 more minutes. Remove the fish and keep warm. Beat together the egg, sugar and vinegar. Add the beaten-egg mixture to the onions, garlic and chillies in the pan. Keep the heat very low and stir constantly as you don't want it to curdle . When the sauce is thickened, spoon it over the fish. Sprinkle over the ground cummin and coriander leaves and serve hot.

Coriander Baked Fish (Pakki Hui Machli)

2 fish, about 1 kg each (or one big one)
Salt to taste
2½ T oil or ghee
2½ T finely chopped garlic
2 fresh green chillies, seeded and chopped
2 t fresh grated ginger
2 T fresh chopped coriander
2½ t coriander seeds
1 t brown sugar
1 t turmeric

½ t black mustard seeds
½ t fenugreek seeds
2½ t salt
6 T lemon juice
6 T ghee or oil
½ c onion, finely chopped
4 fresh tomatoes, skinned and chopped
1 t garam masala
2 T fresh chopped coriander for garnish

Wash the fish and dry, then sprinkle its insides with salt. Preheat oven to 215°C.

Blend the garlic, chillies, ginger, fresh coriander, coriander seeds, sugar, turmeric, mustard seeds, fenugreek, salt and lemon juice into a smooth paste. Fry the onions in 1 T oil until golden. Add the ground and blended paste and continue to fry until the mixture thickens. Stir in the fresh tomatoes and the garam masala. Prepare a baking-dish by spreading about 1½ T oil or ghee over the bottom and sides. Spread a third of the masala mixture over one side of the fish, and place the fish, with this side down, in the dish. Fill the inside of the fish with one third of the masala mixture and secure it with skewers or sew it up. Spread the remaining third of the masala over the top of the fish and cover the dish with a tight lid or aluminium foil. Bake for about 25 minutes. Brown the fish slightly under the grill before serving it garnished with the fresh chopped coriander.

All fish are much better cooked whole than in pieces.
— Maestro Martino, 1450-75

Fish Kebab (Machli Kabab)

1 kg firm fish steaks
Lemon juice
1 t ground cummin
½ t chilli powder
1 t garam masala

Salt
1 cup yoghurt
2 onions, quartered
1 capsicum, sliced
Ghee, melted

Wash the fish and cut into chunks to fit on to the skewers. Smear with lemon juice and a little salt to taste. Beat the cummin, chilli and garam masala into the yoghurt. Put the fish chunks into this mixture and stir round to get them well covered. Marinate for an hour. Arrange the chunks on skewers, alternating with the onions and capsicum. Baste well with the melted ghee and grill gently until tender.

You can cook this dish in the oven if you wish, but the smoky taste of the open fire is for me.

Poultry and Egg Dishes

Poultry is expensive in India, and is normally only eaten on special occasions — unless you are rich, of course. Nevertheless, poultry is extremely popular. The native chickens tend to be small, hardy and agile, and it's their agility which probably makes them a bit stringy. We are lucky in the West to have frozen chickens. They cook quickly and often absorb more flavour than the fresh variety because the freezing process tends to break down tissue and make them more tender.

Despite the expense, India has hundreds of delicious recipes for poultry. Some are simple creations, creamy with yoghurt or coconut milk, others are rich, roasted and redolent with spices. Sometimes the fowl is fiery and at other times it emerges in sauces of crushed almonds or cashews. But barbecued, curried, roasted or baked, it's all delicious when presented with the subtle flavours and spices used by clever Indian cooks.

Probably the most famous Indian chicken dish is Tanduri Chicken, a product of the special clay oven found in the north of India. These renowned ovens resemble the giant jars within which the naughty villains hid from Ali Baba. The tandur is usually sunk into the ground, but if built above the ground, it is heavily insulated with a thick layer of plaster. A charcoal fire on the flat bottom heats this tandur to scorching point about half way up, above which it glows with a heat which diminishes towards the neck. The cook has to light the fire about two hours before he or she starts work. Apart from chicken, lamb kebabs and breads all emerge from this magnificent device with distinctive zest. Tradition has it that the well-used tandur will improve everything cooked in it, because the clay releases a distinct fragrance of its own, compounded with the aromatic memories of the smoke from a hundred different marinades dripping on the coals.

Food cooked in the tandur is marinated for at least four hours before being impaled on long iron skewers. The skewers are then lowered into the oven with the tips resting on the coals and the food positioned about 35 cm above the surface of the heat. The food is withdrawn every few minutes to be basted with melted ghee and its marinade. The heat is intense and a chicken is cooked in about twenty minutes.

TO PREPARE CHICKEN FOR CURRIES

For curries, chickens are chopped up into smaller pieces than is usual in most Western dishes, to allow greater penetration of the spices. The method is:

Joint the chicken. Chop the thighs in two. Divide the breast into two, then chop in half, giving you four pieces. Divide the wings into two, cutting at the first joint and leaving the wing tip attached to the second. Chop the back into four pieces (not counted as eating material because there's no meat on them). The neck and giblets are utilised in much the same way as we do.

POULTRY

Tanduri Chicken (Tandoori Murgha)

There are almost as many recipes for this dish as there are people who cook 'it, but there are one or two fundamentals that remain the same. The birds should be small, about spring-chicken size, they should be skinned, and they should be marinated. Since most of us don't have a tandur, the next best thing is the barbecue. Although you won't be using the skewer in the same way as in the tandur, it's not a bad idea to thrust it lengthways through the chickens anyway, as the heat is conducted along the metal and reduces the cooking time by assisting from the inside. This dish can also be cooked in the kitchen oven.

2 chickens, about 500 g each

Skin the chickens and cut slits in the flesh to allow the marinade to penetrate.

Marinade 1

1 cup yoghurt
2 t salt
2 t crushed garlic
2 t freshly grated ginger
1 t white pepper

½ t chilli powder
1 t garam masala
Red food colouring (optional)
Ghee for oven method of cooking

Combine the yoghurt with all the ingredients except the ghee, and rub this marinade all over the chickens, both inside and out. Leave, covered, for at least 4 hours, or overnight in the fridge.

Get a good glowing fire on the barbecue, and when the thin white ash appears on the surface, start your cooking. Put the chickens on a rack above the fire, turning to ensure they cook all round. To test if the birds are cooked, pierce the thighs with the point of a small knife. The juice that runs out should be pale yellow.

If cooking in the oven, preheat it to 200°C. Melt the ghee in a roasting pan and put the chickens in the pan side by side, breasts down. Spoon ghee over them and cook for 20 minutes. Turn them on one side and cook for 15 minutes, then repeat the process for the other side. For the final 10-15 minutes, turn the birds breast upwards and baste every 5 minutes. Serve bedded in a salad, or on a large dish with the salad ingredients arranged around them.

You can use the Tanduri Mix in the marinade, of course. (*See* p. 22) About 3 t is sufficient for this recipe.

Marinade 2

1 c vinegar
2½ c yoghurt
2 large onions, chopped
4 crushed cloves garlic
1 lemon
2 t garam masala

1 t chilli powder
1 t paprika
Red or yellow food colouring
  (optional)
1½ t salt

Blend all the ingredients into a marinade and proceed as above.

Hyderabad Chicken (Murgha Hyderabad)

1 t turmeric	6 black peppercorns
1 c yoghurt	5 cm cinnamon stick, broken
3 T ghee or oil	3 cardamom pods
1 medium onion, sliced	4 cloves
1 ½ t fresh grated ginger	1 chicken, about 1.5 kg, cut into pieces
6 crushed cloves garlic	Salt
2 fresh green chillies, seeded and chopped	500 g tomatoes, peeled and chopped

Stir the turmeric into the yoghurt. Fry the onion until golden. Add the rest of the spices and stir-fry for another 2 or 3 minutes. Add the chicken pieces and fry for a further 2 minutes. Put in the tomatoes and salt to taste and pour over the yoghurt. Cover and simmer gently until the chicken is tender.

Chicken in Almond-cream Sauce (Murgha Jalfraise)

1 large onion, minced	5 cm cinnamon stick, broken
4 T ghee or oil	2 T yoghurt
1 clove crushed garlic	2 large tomatoes, peeled and seeded
1 ½ t fresh ground ginger	650 g Tanduri-cooked chicken
2 T fine ground almonds or cashews	3 T ghee
1 t turmeric powder	1 red chilli, seeded and sliced
1 t chilli powder	1 seeded capsicum, sliced into squares
1 t ground cummin	3 T blanched slivered almonds
2 t ground coriander	1 tomato, chopped
4 cloves	¼ ~ ½ c thick cream
6 cardamoms	2 hard-boiled eggs, sliced

Fry onion, garlic and ginger for about 4 minutes. Add the ground nuts and all the spices and stir-fry for another 4 minutes. Stir in the yoghurt and a little water and add the finely chopped, peeled and seeded tomatoes. Simmer for 15 minutes. Debone the chicken and cut into strips 5 cm long. Fry in ghee for 3 or so minutes. Add the chilli and capsicum cut into squares, together with the almonds and the chopped tomato. Simmer for 5 minutes. Stir in the cream and add the sliced eggs. Serve warm.

Sultana Chicken (Kishmish Murgha)

1.5 kg chicken, in pieces	2 cloves crushed garlic
Salt	2 t fresh grated ginger
Ghee	1 T tamarind water (or vinegar)
½ c almonds, chopped and blanched	2 T brown sugar
½ c sultanas	3-6 parboiled potatoes, quartered
2 medium onions, sliced	1 c green peas
2 red chillies	

Wash the chicken well and sprinkle with salt, then fry it until it's nicely browned. Heat a little more ghee and fry the nuts and sultanas. Set aside. Now fry the onions, garlic and ginger until the onions are golden. Put in the chicken pieces, add the tamarind water or vinegar, sugar, potatoes and peas. Simmer gently until the chicken is tender. Stir in nuts and sultanas and serve.

Spiced Fried Chicken (Murgha Khandan)

$\frac{1}{4}$ c water
1.5 kg chicken, in pieces
1 t fine chopped garlic
Salt
1 t fresh grated ginger
1 t ground cardamom
Pinch nutmeg
Ground black pepper

3 T ghee
1 fresh green chilli, seeded and
  chopped
$\frac{1}{2}$ c ground cashews or almonds
A few boiled vegetables (Carrot sticks,
  peas, cauliflower sprigs, etc)
Sliced hard-boiled eggs
Sliced tomatoes

Combine garlic, ginger and ground spices into a paste with salt, and smear over the chicken pieces. Let stand for at least 30 minutes.

Fry the chicken pieces in a pan until they are brown. Add the cashews or almonds and stir-fry for about 2 minutes, then add about $\frac{1}{4}$ c water. Cover and simmer for about 10 minutes until the meat is tender. Put the chicken pieces in a heated serving dish. Add the boiled vegetables to the pan and toss these in the spicy gravy. Surround the chicken with the vegetables and gravy and garnish with the hard-boiled eggs and tomato.

Creamed Tomato Chicken and Fresh Fruit (Murgha Baghdadi)

500 g deboned chicken breasts, or
  thighs
$\frac{1}{4}$ c ghee
4 large tomatoes, peeled, seeded
  and pulped
1 scant T tomato purée
$\frac{1}{4}$ t chilli powder
2-3 t lemon juice
Sugar and salt to taste

White pepper
4 T thick cream
2 T chopped fresh coriander
2 hard-boiled eggs, sliced
12 blanched and slivered almonds
About $\frac{1}{2}$ c diced fresh fruit (mango,
  pineapple, pear, apple, banana)
4 or 5 ripe pitted cherries

Cut the chicken into 5 cm cubes and fry until almost cooked through. Set aside and keep warm. Sauté the tomato pulp and purée for about 5 minutes. Stir in the chilli, lemon juice, sugar, salt and pepper. Cook for a further 10 minutes on a moderate heat. If the mixture becomes too thick, add a little chicken stock or water. Stir in the cream and add the chicken pieces. Cook on a low heat for about 4 minutes, add the fruit, coriander, egg slices, almonds and the cherries. Heat through and serve.

Chicken Korma (Murgha Korma)

Ghee for frying
2 medium onions, finely chopped
6 crushed cloves garlic
One third c yoghurt
2 bay leaves
Salt to taste
1.5 kg chicken, in pieces
250 g tomatoes, peeled and sliced
1 T lemon juice

2 c water
4 cloves
8 black peppercorns
1 t fresh grated ginger
1 t ground cummin
1 t ground cardamom
5 cm stick of cinnamon, broken
1 t chilli powder
1 t garam masala

Fry onion until golden. Set aside half. To the remaining onion add all the spices except the garam masala, together with the ginger, garlic, bay leaves, yoghurt and salt. Stir over a low heat for 5 minutes, add the chicken pieces and simmer for a further 5 minutes. Add the garam masala, tomatoes and lemon juice and finally stir in the water. Cover and simmer for 30-40 minutes until the chicken is cooked. Garnish with the reserved fried onions.

Roast Chicken Kashmiri (Dum Murgha Kashmir)

1.5 kg roasting chicken
2 t fresh grated ginger
2 T lemon juice
Salt to taste
1 t sugar
1 T fresh chopped coriander

8 cloves crushed garlic
2 green chillies, seeded and finely
   chopped
1 t Kashmir Garam Masala (See p. 20)
½ c yoghurt
2 t rose water

Grind together into a smooth paste ½ t Kashmir Garam Masala and all the above ingredients except the rose water and coriander. Smear the chicken well with this and leave for at least 3 hours to absorb the spices. Now prepare roasting paste as follows:

Roasting Masala Paste

6 T ghee
2 large onions, minced
4 cloves crushed garlic
1½ t fresh ground ginger
6 cloves
6 black peppercorns
1 t cummin seeds

2 t coriander seed
4 cardamom pods
1 t fennel seeds
4 T ground almonds
Salt
Pinch powdered nutmeg
2 T water

Fry the onions, garlic and ginger in half the ghee, until the onions are cooked. Roast all the spices (and the almonds), then grind to a fine powder. Add to the onion mixture and stir-fry for 4 minutes. Melt the remaining ghee and fry the chicken, turning to brown evenly. Remove from the pan and allow to cool. Then smear thoroughly with the roasting masala. Place in a pan with a tight-fitting lid, together with 2 T water. Put into a preheated oven (200°C.) and cook for about 40 minutes until the chicken is done. (Don't open the pan during this time as the steam must be kept in to moisten the fowl.)

While the chicken is roasting mix together the rose water and remaining $\frac{1}{2}$ t of Kashmir Masala, and prepare the chopped coriander garnish. When the chicken is cooked, remove the lid and pour the rose water mixture over the bird. Cook for a further 3-4 minutes to evaporate any liquid in the pan, scatter over the coriander and serve.

Chicken Dhansak (Murgha Dhansak)

$\frac{3}{4}$ **c channa dhal**
$\frac{3}{4}$ **c moong dhal**
3$\frac{3}{4}$ c water
2 medium onions, sliced
$\frac{3}{4}$ **c ghee**
2 cloves
3 cloves crushed garlic
1 t fresh ground ginger

1 t garam masala
750 g chicken thighs
1 medium aubergine (eggplant)
2 large tomatoes, peeled, seeded and cut into chunks
250 g spinach
Salt to taste

Wash the dhals well and mix together. Place them in a large saucepan, cover with water and boil gently for about 15 minutes. Melt the ghee meanwhile and fry the sliced onions, cloves, garlic, ginger and garam masala until the onions are done. Next fry the chicken pieces in this mixture, turning well, for about 5 minutes. Take them out and put aside. Cut the aubergine into 2 cm chunks and add these to the masala mix along with the tomatoes and coarsely-chopped spinach. Cook for ten minutes, stirring constantly. Now take the pan of lentils and mash them up in their cooking water, which should be almost totally absorbed. Pour in the vegetable and masala mix, and stir well. Put in the chicken pieces, cover with a tight lid and simmer until the chicken falls off the bone easily.

A justifiably famous Parsee dish. Many dhansaks are complicated to make, and this is just one of the many recipes that exist for this dish.

A master cook — why he's the man among men ... makes citadels
of curious fowls and fish.
— Ben Jonson, 1572-1637

Curried Partridges (Tithar)

6 partridges, each weighing about
   250 g (or any other game birds of
   about the same weight)
Salt
Lemon juice
Livers, hearts and gizzards of the birds
3 T cream
1 t turmeric
4 T ghee
1 ½ T onions, fine chopped

1 t finely chopped garlic
Fresh ground black pepper
1 large onion, chopped
6 cardamom pods, crushed
8 cloves
5 cm stick cinnamon
4 T yoghurt
1 ½ c water
Pinch cayenne pepper or chilli powder

Wash and dry birds. Sprinkle inside and out with lemon juice and salt. Place in large baking dish. Finely chop the gizzards, livers and hearts and set aside. Stir-fry the 1 ½ T finely chopped onion, garlic and black pepper. Add the giblets and fry another 2 or 3 minutes. Remove from pan and mix with the cream and turmeric. Fry the large chopped onion until golden, remove with a slotted spoon and set aside. Add the cardamom, cloves and cinnamon to the pan and fry until the stick breaks up easily and the ghee turns brown. Strain the ghee into the cream and giblet mixture and discard the whole spices. Add the yoghurt and mix well. Smear this cream and yoghurt mixture over the birds. Cover and marinate for about 12 hours. Preheat oven to 200°C, place the birds on a rack in the baking dish and sprinkle over them the marinade together with a little cayenne pepper or chilli powder. Pour half the water down the side of the dish and roast in the centre of the oven for 20 minutes. Turn the heat down a little, add the remaining water and roast for another 30 minutes, basting now and then with the liquid from the pan. Sprinkle the fried onion on top when serving.

Roast Duck with Cashew-nut Stuffing (Vath)

¼ c unsalted cashew nuts
2-2.5 kg duck
Salt
¼ c stale bread cubes, cut about 1 cm
   square
2 hard-boiled eggs, quartered
2 T seedless raisins
1 T fresh chopped coriander
2 T sugar
1 ½ T white vinegar
1 t ground cardamom
Fresh ground black pepper

1 T ghee or oil
1 t ground cummin
½ t aniseed
1 ½ t fresh grated ginger
¼ c finely chopped onion
1 t turmeric
4 crushed cloves garlic
3 large tomatoes, skinned, seeded and
   pulped
1 fresh green chilli, seeded and
   chopped
Chilli powder

Soak the cashews in boiling water for 15 minutes, then drain and chop. Wash and dry the duck, then rub with salt. Chop the giblets finely and fry with the cummin, aniseed, garlic, ginger, onions and salt, until the onions become soft and the mixture starts to brown. Add the cardomom, turmeric, chilli and tomatoes and stir-fry for 3 minutes. Set aside. Thoroughly mix the bread cubes, eggs, raisins, drained nuts, coriander, sugar, vinegar and pepper in a deep bowl. Scrape into this the giblet mixture with as much chilli as you want, and mix thoroughly. Loosely stuff the bird with this mixture, then prick its skin all over at 2.5 cm intervals. Sew up the openings, truss the duck and put it on its side on a rack in a baking dish. Place in a preheated oven (240°C.) and roast for 10 minutes on one side, then for 10 more minutes on the other. Reduce heat to 175°C, turn the bird breast-side up and roast for 1 hour and 40 minutes, basting occasionally. To test if it's cooked, prick the thigh. The juice that runs out should be a clear yellow. If not, cook until it is. Let the duck rest for about 10 minutes before carving.

The same ingredients and method can be used for other birds.

EGG DISHES

Coconut Egg Curry (Narial Anda Kari)

4 large fresh tomatoes, peeled, seeded and pulped	1 t ground coriander
1 c water	1 t turmeric
1 large onion, chopp d	½ t fresh grated ginger
1 clove crushed garlic	6 curry leaves
Ghee or oil	2 cups coconut milk
1 T ground almonds	6-8 hard-boiled eggs, shelled and halved lengthways
1 t chilli powder	

Fry onion until golden, add garlic, ginger, almonds, curry leaves and spices. Stir-fry until browned (3 or 4 minutes.) Add tomatoes and coconut milk and bring to the boil. Turn down heat and simmer about 30 minutes until the mixture thickens. Add the halved eggs, heat through and serve.

Baked Eggs with Shrimp (Pora)

2 fresh green chillies, seeded	10 egg whites
¼ c chopped fresh coriander	5 egg yolks
2 crushed cloves garlic	2 t ground almonds
1 t fresh grated ginger	¼ c peeled shrimps
1 t cummin seeds	Salt to taste
Pinch turmeric powder	Ghee

Blend together everything except the eggs and shrimps. Whisk egg whites, then add the yolks and whisk again. Stir in the blended mixture plus the shrimps and salt to taste. Fry the whole mixture, stirring quickly, until it starts to thicken. Transfer to a baking dish and bake in a preheated oven at 175°C. for 15 minutes, until set.

Eggs with Spinach (Bhaji per Eenda)

1 kg spinach
Ghee
1 small onion, finely chopped
2 cloves crushed garlic
1 t fresh grated ginger

½ t cummin seeds
Chilli powder to taste
Salt and black pepper to taste
½ t garam masala
4 eggs

Prepare spinach and cook in very little water with lid on. Drain and chop. Fry onion, garlic and ginger until golden, add spices and stir-fry for a minute. Add chopped spinach, salt and black pepper to taste. Beat the eggs, pour over the mixture in the pan, cover and cook on low heat until the eggs are set.

Parsi Omelette (Parsi Poro)

4 eggs
1 c diced parboiled potato
Ghee
Salt and pepper to taste
½ t ground cummin

¼ c fresh chopped coriander
½ t garam masala
1 small onion, finely chopped
1 capsicum, chopped and seeded
1 tomato, peeled, seeded and chopped

Fry the potato, onion, capsicum and tomato until they start to brown. Beat eggs gently with the spices. Heat ghee in omelette pan. When the ghee starts to go brown, add the eggs, stirring vigorously with a fork, and moving the pan at the same time. When still moist on top, add the filling, fold and turn out the omelette. Spread a little ghee on top.

Parsi Scrambled Eggs (Ekuri)

6 eggs
½ t salt
2½ T ghee
1 small onion, finely chopped
¼ t turmeric
½ t ground cummin

3 T milk
¼ t ground black peppercorns
1 t scraped, finely chopped fresh ginger
2½ T finely chopped coriander
1½ t finely chopped red or green chillies

Whisk eggs in a bowl. Add milk, salt and black peppercorns and mix in well. (Don't let it get frothy.) Heat ghee in pan until a drop of water splatters in it. Add ginger, fry for 10 seconds, then add onions and fry for 1 minute or so, until they are soft but not brown. Add coriander and turmeric, stirring constantly. Add egg mixture and sprinkle the top with the chopped chillies.

Reduce heat and cook gently, stirring constantly with rubber spatula, until the eggs start to form soft curds. Before serving, sprinkle the top with cummin. You can embellish the dish with wedges of tomatoes or sprigs and leaves of coriander.

Usually eaten with plain parathas or chapatis.

Meat

It's not surprising in the paradoxical mosaic of India, that in this country which is mainly vegetarian is to be found a treasure-house of meat, fowl and fish dishes.

The Hindus, in their pursuit of purity, demand a diet devoid of flesh. To some, not even a blood-coloured vegetable like a tomato or beetroot is acceptable. However, many others eat meat for equally fervent religious reasons, and their particular doctrine will dictate their diet. Jews and Moslems will gorge on goat or mutton but will eschew pork. Christians, on the other hand, chew happily on any kind of meat.

It hasn't always been so. Early Sanscrit writings from 1200 B.C. clearly indicate that meat was commonly eaten, and that of all flesh, beef was a special luxury, for any feast of welcome always included the fatted calf. It has been a source of some embarrassment to sundry religious zealots and political agitators to find out that their revered Vedas don't support their insistence that the cow has always been holy. It was round about the 5th century B.C., when a religious cult centred on Lord Krishna developed, that the deification of this beast emerged. Mystic messages apart, this may well have been a divine intervention on the part of economic common sense, for not only is the cow a gentle creature providing milk and all its associated products, it is also a valuable beast of burden, pulling ploughs and carts, and carrying people. These practical considerations were possibly of more importance to the large agrarian sector than the inclusion of meat in their diet. However, it is true that certain Sanscrit writings of that time contained dire warnings that stated, quite flatly, 'If people eat animals in this world, the animals will eat them in the next.'

From contemporary records and legislation, it is clear, however, that quite a few people continued to eat meat. In the 4th century B.C. for instance, there were superintendents of slaughterhouses with strict instructions about how to run their enterprises, and rigid regulations governing the selling of meat.

Finally meat-eating was abolished in the Hindu religion, but isolated minorities of different religious persuasions continued to consume it.

The Syrian Christians of Malabar, for example, created superb meat dishes. This minority group is a mixture of Syrian settlers and native Indians whose Christianity is a result of Thomas Didymus, one of the Twelve Apostles, coming to India as a missionary in A.D. 52. The Syrian connection is from a group who arrived in A.D. 345 seeking sanctuary from religious persecution. Since cattle were not bred to eat in a predominantly Hindu society, the quality of the beef was poor. Fortunately this inspired the Syrian Christians to triumph over adversity, and they evolved an ingenious and imaginative cuisine based on cubed and minced meat which more than compensated for the poor nature of the raw materials. They also specialise in flamboyantly-spiced duck dishes and have a repertoire of dazzling game recipes.

The Goanese Christians further up the west coast produce noble pork dishes, including the redoubtable vindaloo and a range of spiced sausages very similar to the European

product. Yet another minority, the Parsees, have contributed a battery of great dishes to the culinary scene, notably in the dhansak tradition — meat, fowl or fish cooked in purées of lentils and vegetables.

Of all the minorities, the Muslims are the mightiest meat eaters. The first Muslim invaders were the Moguls who swept down into India in the 8th century A.D. following the route Alexander the Great had used almost 1000 years before. But it wasn't until 1526 that Bakur the Mogul successfully invaded the Punjab and ushered in an era of magnificence, when mosques, palaces, monuments and cities were built all over Northern India. He and his successors became known as the Grand Moguls, exhibiting great elegance and panache in their style of living and creating an architectural tradition that produced the legendary Taj Mahal. Their concern for style and luxury was manifest in more than monuments, for they also bequeathed the truly magnificent Mogul cuisine to India and the world.

An old saying has it that 'You cannot be a good Muslim unless you eat meat and plenty of it.' Pork, of course, was out, the beef poor and difficult to obtain, so they concentrated their considerable talents on the creation of a cuisine based on lamb and goat. But their preoccupation with these particular ungulates didn't prevent them from embellishing their reputation for the most lavish cuisine in India with such dishes as pilaus, birianis, and their famous tandur creations.

In many of the dishes which follow you can substitute beef for mutton. In India, if the meat is likely to be tough, they often either rub it with fresh green pawpaw, or include a piece of green pawpaw in the marinade.

Kashmir Lamb Curry (Kashmiri Rogan Josh)

1 kg boned leg of lamb or mutton	1 T ground coriander
Ghee	1–2 t chilli powder
4 cloves	2 c water
Pinch asafoetida	Pinch saffron strands, toasted
Salt	3 T hot milk
$\frac{1}{2}$ c yoghurt	1–2 t sugar
1 c water	1 T thick cream
$\frac{1}{2}$ t fresh ground ginger	2 cardamoms, peeled and crushed
2 t blanched almonds, chopped fine	1 t Kashmir Garam Masala (See p. 20)

Cut mutton into 2.5 cm cubes. Fry with cloves, asafoetida and salt until well browned all over. Mix the yoghurt with the water and add in little dollops, allowing each dollop to dry up before adding the next. Stir constantly. Sprinkle on the ginger, coriander and chilli, and stir-fry on a high heat for 2 minutes. Pour on the water, bring to the boil uncovered. Reduce the heat to moderate and cook for a further 15 minutes. Meanwhile, grind up the saffron and steep in the hot milk. Stir the sugar and cream into the meat, add the saffron milk, cardamoms and blanched almonds. Cover and simmer until the meat is very tender and the sauce thick. Stir in the garam masala and serve.

MEAT (Lamb)

Kofta Curry (Kofta Kari)

Meat balls

500 g minced meat
6 cloves crushed garlic
½ t fresh grated ginger
Salt to taste

1 ½ large onions, chopped
½ c fresh chopped coriander or mint
1 t garam masala
Oil for deep-frying

Mince together the meat and the onions and mix well with the garlic, coriander or mint, ginger, salt and garam masala. Form the mixture into 2.5 cm balls and deep-fry for 2 minutes. Using a slotted spoon, remove the balls carefully to make sure that they don't fall apart. Set aside.

Sauce

1 t chilli powder
1 t ground cummin
2 t garam masala
2 t paprika
Salt and pepper to taste
Water

Ghee
1 ½ large onions, chopped
2 t paprika
2 T grated fresh ginger
1 ¼ c yoghurt
Lemon juice (optional)

Fry the onions in some ghee until golden. Add the rest of the spices and stir-fry for 3-4 minutes. Spoon in the meat balls and a little water and simmer for 20 minutes or so, gently turning the meat balls and making sure they don't stick to the bottom of the pan. Add the yoghurt and simmer for another 15 or so minutes. Squeeze in some lemon juice before serving if desired.

Lamb Kebabs (Tikka Kebab)

500 g lean lamb, cut into 2.5 cm chunks
3 T vegetable oil
1 medium onion, chopped finely
1 lemon, halved
¼ c chopped fresh ginger
1 t garam masala

1 t paprika
2 T vinegar
Onion rings and lemon wedges for
garnish
Salt to taste
1 ¼ c yoghurt

The secret of this dish is the marination. The kebabs are best cooked over a barbecue, but can be done under a grill.

Mix together the onion and the oil. Rub the lemon over the meat — really get in and strangle the mutton. Now rub the onion and oil mixture all over the meat, and continue strangling for a minute or so to get the chunks really covered. Blend the rest of the ingredients and cover the meat with the mixture. Cover the container and marinate in a cool place for at least 4 hours, or overnight in the fridge.

Thread the meat on to skewers and cook over the barbecue or under the grill until the chunks start to go dark brown. Turn them during the grilling period to ensure they are all cooked uniformly. Garnish with raw onion rings and lemon wedges.

It's best to eat kebabs as soon as they are cooked because they tend to dry out if kept.

Skewered Lamb (Hussaini Kebab)

500 g lean lamb, cut in 2.5 cm pieces
1 crushed clove garlic
1 t grated fresh ginger
2 T finely ground almonds
2 T yoghurt
2 T ground coriander

2 t ground cummin
Salt to taste
2 T sesame oil
2 T lemon juice
Onion rings and lemon wedges for
  garnish

Blend everything except the lamb. Marinate the lamb pieces in the resultant mixture, kneading the mixture well into the meat. Cover and leave for at least 4 hours, or in the fridge for up to 2 days. Cook and serve as for Tikka Kebabs.

Minced Meat Kebabs (Seekh Kebabs)

500 g minced lamb or mutton
1 large onion, finely chopped
2 T finely ground almonds
1 T fresh lemon juice
2 T fresh chopped coriander
1 t garam masala
Freshly ground black pepper
1 T ground coriander

1 t fresh grated ginger
2 T chickpea flour
Salt to taste
1 egg
$\frac{1}{2}$ t roasted poppy seeds
1 T chilli powder
1 t ground cummin
4 T ghee, melted

Garnish
  Lemon wedges
  Tomato quarters

  Onion rings

Mix together all the ingredients except the ghee and the garnish items. Knead the mixture well. Leave it for an hour or so, then divide up into portions. Roll out each portion and shape by hand into a sausage. Thread these on to skewers and cook as for other kebabs, brushing with the ghee as you turn them. Garnish with the lemon, onion and tomato.

Meat after the old usage, beef, mutton, veal to cheer their courage.
— William Forrest, c. 1565

Mutton with Coconut (Baffad)

500 g boned mutton, trimmed and cut into 2.5 cm cubes
5 T desiccated coconut
6 cloves crushed garlic
2 t fresh grated ginger
6 dried chillies, soaked
2 t ground cummin
1 ½ t ground turmeric
2 T ground almonds
Ghee for frying
1 large onion, minced
1 T tamarind water
1 T sugar
4 medium potatoes, peeled and cut into 2.5 cm cubes
3 carrots, peeled and cut into 2.5 cm cubes
1 ½ c water
Salt to taste

Blend and make a paste out of everything except the meat, vegetables, sugar and tamarind water. Fry the paste for about 5 minutes, stirring to prevent sticking. (Very important with coconut as it tends to burn easily.) Stir in the meat and fry for 5 or 6 minutes until it is well coloured. Add tamarind water, sugar and vegetables. Pour in the water, cover and simmer until the vegetables are tender. Add salt to taste.

Lentil and Mutton Stew (Gosht Dhansak)

500 g boned and trimmed mutton, finely diced
1 c channa dhal
1 c moong dhal
3 c water
1 large onion, chopped
6 crushed cloves garlic
1 t fresh grated ginger
6 dried chillies, soaked
1 t ground cummin
1 t ground coriander
2.5 cm cinnamon stick
1 t black peppercorns
2 crushed cardamoms
1 t turmeric powder
2 large tomatoes, seeded and peeled
3 c water
1 medium aubergine, chopped
½ c chopped pumpkin
Bunch spinach
1 T tamarind water
1 T brown sugar

Garnish
1 large onion, cut in rings and fried   Fresh coriander leaves

Wash dhals and mix. Cover with first measure of water and boil gently for about 15 minutes.

Fry onion, garlic, ginger and chillies (drained), stirring for 3 minutes. Grind the spices together, add to the onion mixture and stir fry for another 4 minutes. Add tomatoes and continue to stir fry for another 3 minutes. Now stir in well the finely diced meat and fry for 4 minutes. Set aside.

Mash up lentils and add to the meat and masala mix. Pour in the second measure of water, add the rest of the vegetables and salt to taste. Bring to the boil, then simmer, covered, until the meat is tender. Lastly stir in the tamarind water and brown sugar. Serve garnished with the fried onion rings and chopped fresh coriander leaves.

Traditionally this dish is eaten with brown rice by the Parsees.

Meat and Spinach Curry (Palak Gosht)

500 g lean trimmed mutton in 2.5 cm cubes
500 g spinach, washed and chopped
1 large onion
1 T fresh grated ginger
5 cloves crushed garlic
Ghee for frying

½ t black cummin seeds
4 dried red chillies
Salt to taste
3 bay leaves
3 crushed cardamom pods
½ c yoghurt
Pepper to taste

Blend onion, garlic, ginger and chillies. (Take the seeds out of the chillies if you don't want it so hot.) Blend to a smooth purée, adding a little water if needed to get it really smooth. Heat the oil and fry the cummin seeds for 1 minute. Add the blended mixture and stir-fry until it browns. (About 10 minutes.) Add the meat and stir well to get it covered. Cook, covered, on low heat until the juices start from the meat, then uncover and cook until the juice is almost all absorbed. Put in the spinach, salt, bay leaves and crushed cardamoms. Cook until the liquid that comes from the spinach is absorbed, which should take about an hour. The meat should be tender by this time. Remove from the heat, stir in the yoghurt and pepper, and serve.

Kidney Curry (Gurda Kari)

4 lambs' kidneys
2 medium onions, chopped
2 cloves crushed garlic
3 large tomatoes, seeded and peeled
Oil for frying
1 t garam masala

1 t turmeric powder
1 t ground cummin
1 t ground coriander
A few bay leaves
Salt to taste

Wash, trim and quarter the kidneys. Fry onions until golden, add the garlic, ginger, tomatoes, spices and salt and stir-fry for 10 minutes. Put in the kidneys and cook until tender. Garnish with tomato wedges.

Mutton Madras (Madrasi Gosht)

500 g lean trimmed mutton in chunks
Ghee or oil for frying
1 large onion, chopped
2 t garam masala
2 t chilli powder

Generous ¼ c tomato purée
4 cardamoms
Salt to taste
1 T lemon juice

Fry the mutton to seal it. Remove the meat and fry the onion for a couple of minutes, then add the garam masala and chilli powder. Stir-fry for about 4 minutes. Now return to the pan the mutton pieces plus the tomato purée and crushed cardamoms. Stir well and add a close-fitting lid. Simmer gently for 30 minutes, stirring from time to time. Add a little water if the sauce seems to be getting too thick (though it ought to be quite thick). Finally, when the meat is tender, add the salt and the lemon juice, stir and serve.

Spiced Leg of Lamb (Raan)

2.5 kg leg of lamb
1 c hot water

$\frac{1}{2}$ **t saffron threads**
2 T boiling water

Marinade 1

1 $\frac{1}{2}$ t fresh grated ginger
$\frac{1}{2}$ **t cardamom seeds**
8 cloves
1 t ground coriander
1 t chilli powder
3 T lemon juice

6 cloves crushed garlic
2.5 cm cinnamon stick, crushed
1 t ground cummin
1 t turmeric powder
Salt to taste

Blend all the marinade ingredients into a smooth purée. Make a dozen slashes 2.5 cm long and twice as deep over the surface of the lamb leg. Smear over this the purée, getting as much as possible into the slashes. Set aside to marinate for at least 30 minutes.

Marinade 2

4 T unsalted, unroasted pistachio nuts
2 t slivered, blanched almonds
1 c yoghurt

4 T seedless raisins
Scant $\frac{1}{2}$ c honey

Blend the nuts, raisins and yoghurt into a smooth purée. Spread evenly over the lamb. Put the leg in a casserole, drip over the honey and cover with a tightly-fitting lid. Marinate in a cool place for 12 hours, or in the fridge for at least 48 hours.

Preheat the oven to 175°C. Soak the saffron in the 2 T boiling water for 15 minutes. Pour the saffron and its water over the leg of lamb and put another cup of water down the sides of the casserole. Bring to the boil over a high heat, cover tightly and bake in the middle of the oven for 1 $\frac{1}{2}$ hours. Reduce the heat to 120°C and cook for another 30 min. Let the lamb set in the gravy for about half an hour before carving.

Curried Brains (Bheja Rasedaar)

4 brains
1 T lemon juice
Water
Ghee for frying
1 large onion, finely chopped
2 tomatoes, peeled, seeded and
chopped
2 t ground coriander

2 t cummin
1 t turmeric
1 t garam masala
4 bay leaves
Chilli powder to taste
$\frac{3}{4}$ **c yoghurt**
Tomato wedges and chopped fresh
coriander for garnish

Wash and halve the brains. Put in a pot with lemon juice and enough water to cover. Simmer for 15 minutes. Set aside.

Fry the onions until golden, add the spices, tomatoes, and bay leaves and fry for another 3-4 minutes, stirring. Strain the brains (reserving the liquid), and add them to the mixture, stir-frying until they are well covered by the sauce. Now pour in the liquid in which the brains were cooked and simmer until the meat is tender, about 20-30 minutes. Add the yoghurt, stir well and serve. Garnish with the tomato wedges, and sprinkle over the coriander.

Liver Curry (Kaleji Kari)

500 g liver, diced
2 large onions, finely chopped
2 t fresh grated ginger
2 fresh chillies, seeded and chopped
2 t ground coriander
2 t crushed garlic

1 t ground cummin
½ t chilli powder
½ c beef broth (from cube)
1 c coconut milk
1 t grated lemon rind
Salt to taste

Fry onions, ginger, garlic and chillies, stirring, until the onions are golden. Stir in well the coriander, cummin and chilli powder. Add the liver until the colour changes, stirring to prevent sticking, then pour in the coconut milk and broth, and cook uncovered until the liver is tender and the gravy has thickened. Stir in the lemon rind and serve.

Beef or Mutton Dopiazah

This is a Muslim dish. Historically, Hindus don't eat onions, garlic or meat. Strict Brahmans still won't touch onions or garlic, as it is reputed to heat the blood and encourage unbridled passions. The literal meaning of Dopiazah, do piazza, or even doopiafa, is 'two onions', and you'll notice in all these recipes there are in fact two quantities of onions. Newly-converted Muslims embrace these dishes with fervour but may find their passions remain bridled unless their unbridled sport is concluded with somebody who has an equal love of onions!

4 large onions, thinly sliced
¾ c ghee
500 g beef or mutton, cubed
1 t chilli powder
4 cloves garlic, crushed
2 c plain yoghurt
1 t ground ginger
1 t salt

1 t cummin seed
4 cloves
6 black peppercorns
4 cardamoms
½ t ground cinnamon
1 t garam masala
6 tomatoes, peeled and halved
Chopped fresh coriander

Heat ghee and fry one onion until golden brown. Remove the rings from the ghee and set aside for garnish. Take the cubed meat and sauté in the onion-flavoured ghee until sealed on all sides. Remove and set aside. Add cummin, cloves, peppercorns, cardamoms and cinnamon to pan and stir well. Add remaining onions along with yoghurt, ginger and salt. Cook for 2 minutes, then add meat and mix in well. Cover and simmer gently for 1½ hours or until meat is tender. (Add water if mixture becomes too dry.) Now add the tomatoes, then sprinkle with the garam masala and fresh coriander. Cover and simmer for a further 20 minutes. Serve garnished with the onion rings.

All flesh is grass, and all the goodness thereof.
— Isaiah

MEAT (Beef)

Curried Roast Beef (Masaledar Raan)

2.5 kg boned rolled sirloin beef	**1 t fresh ground black pepper**
3 T lemon juice	**½ t chilli powder**
2½ T coarse salt	**1½ T ghee**

Combine the lemon juice, salt, pepper and chilli, and rub firmly all over the joint. With a long skewer perforate the meat at 2.5 cm intervals, piercing the roast right through each time. Smear the ghee all over it and set aside for 15 minutes or so.

Masala

2 t saffron threads	**8 cloves**
3 T boiling water	**2.5 cm cinnamon stick, crushed**
1 medium onion, chopped	**½ t cardamom seeds**
3 T yoghurt	**½ t coriander seeds**
3 crushed cloves garlic	**½ t cummin seeds**
2 T fresh grated ginger	**3 T melted ghee**
3 t black mustard seeds	

Soak saffron threads in boiling water for 10 minutes. Blend everything else into a smooth purée, then stir in the saffron and its water and mix well. Smear the masala over the joint with your fingers and perforate as before. Marinate at room temperature for 12 hours, or in the fridge overnight, covered.

Preheat the oven to 230°C. Place beef on rack in roasting tin in the middle of the oven. After 15 minutes reduce the heat to 175°C. Roast the beef until it's well done: 170°F on a meat thermometer. (If you haven't got one, reckon 60 minutes to the kilogram, starting from the time you turn down the oven to the lower heat.) Carve into 8 mm thick slices and serve swiftly.

Minced Beef Curry (Gaay Gosht Keema)

500 g minced beef	**1 c water**
1 large onion, finely chopped	**4 cloves**
4 crushed cloves garlic	**4 crushed cardamoms**
4 or 5 bay leaves	**1 t garam masala**
Oil or ghee for frying	**1 t turmeric powder**
1 T fresh grated ginger	**Chilli powder to taste**
3 T yoghurt	**Salt to taste**
3 T tomato purée	**Chopped fresh coriander for garnish**

Fry onions, garlic, bay leaves and cloves, until the onion is golden. Add ginger, tomato purée, yoghurt and remaining spices and stir-fry for 5 minutes. Add the mince and fry, stirring well, for 5 minutes. Add water and salt to the pan, cover, and simmer for about an hour. The dish should be moist but without too much gravy. If it's too liquid at the end, cook over high heat to evaporate the excess. Garnish with chopped coriander. You can add peas to this dish if you wish.

Pork Vindalu

A vindalu, or vindaloo, is originally a Goanese dish, perfected in the South. It is normally very hot and sour; in fact it is the hottest curry in the southern repertoire, where hot curries are hotter than anywhere else. Talk about stirring a sluggish liver!

1 T coriander seed	1 t chilli powder
¹/₂ t cummin seed	1 t salt
1 green cardamom	Vinegar
2.5 cm stick cinnamon	500 g pork, cubed
3 cloves	4 bay leaves, broken
1 t turmeric powder	¹/₂ c ghee
2 t ginger, finely chopped	3 cloves garlic, finely chopped
1 t mustard seeds	

Lightly roast coriander and cummin seed and add to cardamom, cinnamon, cloves, peppercorns, turmeric, ginger, chilli powder and salt. Grind together, adding a little vinegar to form a paste.

Wash pork cubes in a weak solution of vinegar. Drain and add to masala paste, stirring well to ensure each piece is well covered. Sprinkle with bay leaves and cover with vinegar. Leave to marinate overnight if possible.

Heat ghee and dry garlic until it turns golden. Add mustard seeds and fry until they pop. Now add pork and the marinade and cook gently until meat is tender. If more liquid is required, add vinegar. (Water should never be used for a vindalu.)

MEAT (Pork)

Vegetables

The vegetarian cuisine of India is supreme — which isn't surprising when you consider that millions of people have been refining it for thousands of years.

Undoubtedly their art has been fostered by the vast array of raw materials available to them. Peas, beans, lentils and all the leguminous vegetables provide a major source of protein in any vegetarian diet, and in India the choice is staggering. (For example, Northern India alone produces over 60 varieties of lentils — red, green, black or yellow; husked or unhusked; large, small, flat or heart-shaped — this list goes on. Each will have characteristic properties absolutely essential for a particular dish.) This profusion of vegetables and fruit, the enormous variety of rice and other grains, coupled with vast regional differences and the aforementioned centuries of tradition, have all contributed to the diversity of this superb cuisine.

While each region has developed certain dishes with their own particular style, character and appeal, it is in the southern and central areas of India that the art flourishes best. The cooking here demonstrates a true understanding of the adventure and refinement that characterises the spirit of this culinary ethic.

The Maharashtrians have possibly developed the most sophisticated cuisine, and a deceptive simplicity masks their extremely subtle skills. Their vegetables are never over-cooked, but retain the natural crispness and colour. The masalas they use merely complement the character of the ingredients, never overpower them. Turmeric is hardly ever used, because it requires a long cooking time and could distort the colour of a dish. Similarly, garam masala is used with great caution, in case it overpowers the delicate balance of the food.

Madras cooking tends to concentrate on a pageant of grain and lentil creations, and where the food of Madras is rich, the Gujarati style tends to be the blandest of all.

One of the most unusual religious minorities in India is the Jains, whose concern with life is so great that they wear veils to avoid killing microbes by swallowing them; they also carry brooms to sweep the ground when they walk, out of their concern for insect life. These people won't eat anything pulled from the earth in case worms or beetles are harmed. But even the Jains' diet can be rich and varied, for to compensate for the forbidden tubers, they have a prodigious range of fruit to enjoy. Dozens of varieties of bananas are always in season, and India grows a whole spectrum of fruits virtually unknown in the West. To most of us a mango is a mango — but not in India. There they will argue the relative merits of half a dozen or more different types. The seasonal variations provide a constantly-changing parade of pineapples, guavas, paw paws, jackfruit, melons and so on, *ad infinitum*, plus all the apples, pears, peaches and plums that the Indians refer to as European fruits.

Limited as we in the West may be, there is still a wide variety of vegetable combinations we can indulge in. (Note, though, that while frozen vegetables have their uses, this isn't one of their areas — unless it's desperation stakes.) Fresh vegetables are best, whether fried, boiled, baked, steamed, puréed or curried. And when you adopt the Indian approach, the bravura you develop will be enormously satisfying both to your ego and your palate — possibly to your soul as well.

There are a number of different techniques that have emerged in this vegetarian cuisine, all with specific names. Any dish with the word dam or dum appearing in it means that the vegetables have been delicately steamed, and retain their shape. Foogaths, on the other hand, are vegetables fried with onions and a little masala, and tarkaris are dishes in which the vegetables have been fried in ghee and then cooked in their own natural juices. Bhartas are virtually purées with the excess moisture dried off.

LENTIL DISHES (Dhals)

For descriptions of the various dhals refer to list of ingredients, p. 14. (Also see Soup, p. 43)

Split Black Peas (Urhad Dhal)

2 c urhad dhal
1 t fresh ground ginger
1 crushed clove garlic
2 fresh green chillies, seeded and
   chopped (optional)
½ t paprika
1 t turmeric powder

Ghee or oil for frying
2 medium onions, chopped
2 medium tomatoes, peeled, seeded
   and chopped
Salt to taste
1 t garam masala
1 t butter

Soak the dhal for a while. Blend the ginger, paprika and turmeric with a drop of water to make a thick paste. Fry the onion until golden, add the paste and stir-fry for 3 minutes, then add the tomatoes and drained dhal. Allow to sizzle, then cover with water, add salt, and cook until tender. Add more water if needed — it depends on the consistency you like. Before serving, add a knob of butter and sprinkle in the garam masala.

Split Yellow Peas (Channa Dhal)

Prepare as in the previous recipe, substituting the dhals in the same proportions.

Split Green Peas (Moong Dhal)

1 c moong dhal
Salt to taste
½ t turmeric powder
Ghee for frying
2 medium onions, chopped

2 cloves crushed garlic
1 t fresh ground ginger
1 t ground cummin
1 t ground coriander
Fresh chopped coriander leaves

Wash and soak dhal for an hour. Drain and boil in a little water with salt and turmeric until soft. Fry the onion, garlic and ginger until soft and golden. Stir in the cummin and coriander and stir-fry for 2 or 3 minutes. Add to the dhal a few minutes before eating. Serve hot garnished with the fresh chopped coriander.

Lentils and Spinach (Dhal Sag)

1½ c mixed lentils
450 g spinach
3 c water
1 t turmeric powder
Salt to taste
½ t chilli powder or to taste

Oil for frying
1 medium onion, chopped
1 t white mustard seeds
1 t cummin seeds
1 t garam masala

Wash dhal and leave to soak. Wash spinach and chop finely. Boil 3 cups of water and add the drained dhal, turmeric, chilli and salt. Cook for 5 minutes and add the spinach. Keep on a moderate heat until the moisture has almost all gone. Meanwhile fry the onions, mustard and cummin seeds until the onion is cooked. Stir into the spinach and dhal with the garam masala. Keep on a moderate heat until cooked. The dish is supposed to be dryish, but add a little water to prevent it sticking. Serve hot.

Gujarati Vegetable Curry (Gujarati Sabzi Kari)

Oil or ghee for frying
500 g par-boiled potatoes, cubed
500 g peas
250 g french beans, sliced
1 medium onion, finely chopped
1 t ground cummin
1 t ground coriander

1 t turmeric powder
1 t paprika
Chilli powder to taste
Salt to taste
1 t brown sugar
½ c water

Fry potatoes, peas and beans. Remove and fry the onion lightly until golden. Stir in all the spices and fry, stirring for a few minutes. Add the vegetables, salt, sugar and about ½ c water. Cover and simmer until the vegetables are cooked.

Vegetable Curry (Gooda Aur Sabzi Ka Kari)

2 medium onions, sliced
3 medium aubergines, chopped or
   sliced
4 large tomatoes
Oil for frying
1 t aniseed
Pinch ground cinnamon
6 curry leaves

Chilli to taste
Pinch turmeric
12 pieces of marrow bone, chopped
   into 5 cm lengths
Few sprigs cauliflower
1 red pepper, seeded and sliced
1 capsicum, seeded and sliced
Salt to taste

Fry the aniseed and cinnamon in the oil for a minute, before adding the onion and curry leaves. When the onion is golden, add the chilli powder, coriander and turmeric. Cook for 5 minutes, add the tomatoes and continue cooking until these are pulpy. Add the bones, aubergines, cauliflower, pepper and capsicum. Season with salt and pepper and simmer until the vegetables are tender.

Readily available vegetables can be substituted for those not in season, e.g. use sliced potatoes instead of the aubergine. Or add peas if you wish.

Stuffed Capsicums (Aloo Mirchi)

4 large capsicums
Fresh chopped coriander

½ t garam masala

Stuffing
500 g potatoes, boiled and cubed
Oil for frying
½ t cummin seeds
½ t garam masala
1 medium onion, finely chopped

2 fresh green chillies, seeded and chopped
1 T chopped peanuts
Salt to taste
Fresh ground black pepper

Sauce
1 large onion, coarsely chopped
1 large tomato, peeled and coarsely chopped
2 cloves crushed garlic

1 t fresh chopped ginger
2 fresh chillies, seeded and chopped
About 4 T oil
½ c hot water

Slice the top off the capsicums and remove the pith and seeds. Dip in boiling water to soften for a minute. Set aside.

Make the filling by frying the onions and chillies until the onion is golden. Add nuts and fry a further minute, stir in the spices for a minute, then add the potatoes and fry for 5 minutes. Stir in salt and pepper and mix. The potatoes should be soft, but not mushy. Stuff the capsicums with this mixture, using the handle of a teaspoon to fill them thoroughly.

Now the sauce. Blend onion, tomato, ginger, garlic and fresh chillies. Heat oil and fry the filled capsicums, turning them gently until almost done. Remove to a plate and add the blended mixture to the oil in the pan. Fry the mixture until it thickens, add the hot water, cover and simmer for about 3 or 4 minutes. Then lay the capsicums in the center, sprinkle with garam masala and cook for another 5 minutes. Garnish with fresh chopped coriander.

Peas with Fresh Cheese (Matar Panir)

You can make your own panir as described in the ingredients list on p. 13, or you can use ready-made ricotta cheese.

2 cups cheese cubes about 2.5 cm in size
Oil or ghee for frying
1 t fresh grated ginger
1 t turmeric powder
Chilli to taste
1 t cummin seeds
2 crushed cardamoms
2.5 cm crushed cinnamon stick
2 medium onions, finely chopped

1 t mustard seeds
1 t poppy seeds
Salt to taste
2 c peas
4 tomatoes, chopped
2 c water
1 t garam masala
1 T lemon juice

Fry the cheese cubes until golden. Remove and drain. Blend the ginger, turmeric, chilli, cummin, cardamom and cinnamon into a paste, using a little water. Fry the onion, mustard and poppy seeds until golden, add the paste and salt, and stir-fry for another 3 minutes. Add the peas and tomatoes, stir for a minute, add water and cook until tender. Before serving, sprinkle with garam masala and lemon juice.

Courgette and Onion (Torai Do Piazza)

1 kg courgettes, peeled
Oil for frying
2 large onions, sliced
2 crushed cloves garlic
Salt to taste

2 tomatoes, peeled and chopped
**1 fresh green chilli, seeded and
  chopped**
$\frac{1}{2}$ t garam masala

Fry the onions and garlic until golden. Mix in chilli and garam masala and stir fry for a minute. Add the tomatoes and fry for about 2 minutes, then stir in well the courgettes. Reduce the heat to a simmering temperature, cover the pan and cook for about 10 minutes.

Potato and Green Bananas (Patiya)

450 g potatoes, cubed
**250 g green bananas, peeled and
  sliced**
Salt to taste
Fresh ground black pepper

2 cups water
Scant $\frac{1}{2}$ c desiccated coconut
A few curry leaves
2 t mustard seeds
Oil or ghee for frying

Boil the potatoes and bananas until nearly done, with salt. Add the coconut and cook for another 5 minutes. Heat the oil or ghee and fry the curry leaves and mustard seeds. When the seeds begin to jump, pour them into the patiya. Serve with another curry.

Steamed Spiced Cauliflower (Dum Gobi)

1 small cauliflower
Oil or ghee for frying
Salt and pepper to taste
$\frac{1}{2}$ c chopped cashews

2 t sunflower seeds
$\frac{1}{2}$ t garam masala
$\frac{1}{2}$ t fresh grated ginger

Steam the cauliflower until half cooked. Put in an oven dish, spread with butter or ghee, cover and bake in a moderate oven, 180°C, until tender. Remove and brown under griller. Lightly fry the nuts, seeds and ginger, mix in the spice and sprinkle over the cauliflower. Serve hot.

Cauliflower is nothing but a cabbage with a college education.
— Mark Twain, 1835-1910

Steamed Green Beans (Phali Dum)

About 1 t oil or ghee
½ c water
340 g french or string beans
1 medium onion, sliced

½ t fresh grated ginger
Salt to taste
½ t fennel seeds

Boil the water and the ghee. Add the beans, onion and seasoning. Mix well, cover, and cook until the beans are tender but firm. If there's any moisture left, drive it out by raising the heat. Sprinkle in the fennel seeds and serve.

Fried Pumpkin (Kaddu Foogath)

Oil or ghee for frying
1 medium onion, sliced
½ t fresh grated ginger
2 cloves crushed garlic

½ t chilli powder, or to taste
500 g pumpkin, peeled and cubed
1 T lemon juice
Salt to taste

Fry onion lightly. Blend garlic, ginger and chilli to a paste. Stir this into the onion with the pumpkin, lemon juice and salt. Add a little water and cook until tender.

Fried Green Bananas (Kela Foogath)

6 green bananas
½ t fresh grated ginger
4 cloves crushed garlic
½ t cummin seeds
Chilli to taste

About 4 T ghee
1 medium onion, sliced
Salt to taste
Scant ½ c desiccated coconut

Peel the bananas and soak in water for half an hour. Grind the ginger, garlic, cummin and chilli into a paste. Lightly fry the onion, add the paste and fry for a few minutes. Add the drained banana pieces, and salt, and stir fry. When half cooked, stir in the desiccated coconut and cook until the bananas are tender.

Sautéed Beans and Coconut (Bean Foogath)

3 T ghee
2 t black mustard seed
1 bay leaf
3 cm dried hot peppers

½ c grated coconut
Salt and pepper
500 g beans, cut into 3 cm pieces

Steam beans for 7-8 minutes. Fry mustard seed, bay leaf and crumbled hot peppers until mustard seeds pop. Add the beans and stir-fry for 2-3 minutes. Mix in coconut and toss the mixture well.

Sautéed Cabbage and Coconut (Cabbage Foogath)

5 T ghee	½ t paprika
2 medium onions, finely chopped	1 shredded cabbage
2 cloves garlic, finely chopped	1 t salt
2.5 cm piece of finely chopped ginger	½ c grated coconut

Fry onion, paprika and ginger in ghee. Add cabbage and sprinkle with salt. Stir. When almost cooked, stir in coconut and continue frying until tender.

You can cook many other vegetables in this fashion.

Eggplant and Potato Curry (Tamatar Alu Bhaji Tarkari)

2 small eggplants, cubed	3 T mustard oil
2 large potatoes, peeled and diced	2 t fresh ginger
2 large ripe tomatoes, peeled and chopped	1 t ground cummin seed
	½ t turmeric powder
1 large onion, finely chopped	1 t soft brown sugar
2 fresh chillies, seeded and chopped	Salt to taste
1 bunch of spinach	

Wash and remove tough stalks from spinach and roughly chop. Heat oil until very hot. Fry potatoes until golden and remove. Fry eggplant until golden and remove. Fry onion until golden, add ginger, cummin and turmeric and stir-fry for 1 minute. Add chillies, tomatoes and salt, then add potatoes, eggplant and spinach. Stir, cover and cook on a low heat until the spinach is soft, adding a little water if needed. Now add sugar and cook uncovered, stirring from time to time, until the liquid has gone.

Green Pepper and Tomato Curry (Mirch Tamatar Tarkari)

About 3 T ghee	Black pepper
225 g green pepper, sliced	450 g tomatoes, peeled and chopped
1 t fresh grated ginger	Fresh coriander leaves, chopped
Salt to taste	½ t garam masala

Fry green pepper, ginger, salt and a pinch of pepper for 3 or 4 minutes. Add the tomatoes, salt and sugar. Stir-fry on a higher heat for 5 minutes. Sprinkle with garam masala and coriander.

My vegetable love should grow vaster than empires.
— Andrew Marvel, 1621-78

Carrot and Radish Purée (Gajjar muli bharta)

225 g carrots, peeled, trimmed and chopped
225 g radishes, peeled, trimmed and chopped
½ t fresh grated ginger

1 medium onion, finely chopped
Salt to taste
½ t garam masala
½ t paprika
2 tomatoes, chopped

Boil carrots and radishes in a minimum of water until soft, then mash. Fry onion and ginger until golden. Add the mashed vegetables, salt, garam masala, paprika and tomatoes. Mix well and cook until the juice has gone.

Eggplant Purée (Baigan Bharta)

2 medium eggplants
Oil for frying
2 medium onions, chopped
1 t ground coriander
1 t ground cummin

1 t ground fennel seeds
3 T fresh chopped coriander
Salt to taste
½ t garam masala

Cut each eggplant into quarters, roast until the skin blackens and puckers and the vegetable is soft. Remove skin. Mash or roughly chop. Heat oil and fry onion until golden. Add spices and stir-fry for 1 minute. Add tomatoes, eggplant, fresh coriander and salt and cook uncovered on a low heat until the liquid evaporates. Sprinkle in garam masala and stir well for a minute or so. Serve hot or cold.

Potato and Peas Curry (Aloo Matar Rasa)

1 large onion, finely chopped
1 fresh chilli, seeded and chopped
2 t fresh grated ginger
Oil for frying
½ t turmeric powder
2 t ground coriander
1 c peas
1 c chicken stock

Salt to taste
500 g potatoes, peeled and cubed
2 large ripe tomatoes, peeled and chopped
3 T yoghurt
1 t garam masala
Fresh chopped coriander for garnish

Blend onion, chilli and ginger into a purée, adding a little water if needed. Fry the blended mixture for 3 or 4 minutes. Add turmeric and coriander and stir-fry for 1 minute. Add peas and chicken stock and cook for about 10 minutes before adding the potatoes. (If the peas are young, add them at the same time.) When the peas and potatoes are half cooked, add the tomatoes, cook for a few more minutes, then stir in the yoghurt. Simmer until the liquid is thick. Just before serving stir in the garam masala and sprinkle over the coriander.

Accompaniments

(SIDE DISHES, SUNDRY PICKLES AND CHUTNEYS)

Chutneys and pickles are an important part of any Indian meal. Their function is almost the same as the ubiquitous sauces and relishes of the West, but they have infinitely more zest and life since many of the chutneys are freshly made for individual meals. In many areas of India, the first task in the morning after lighting the cooking fire is the making of the fresh chutney for the day. Chutneys are not considered as side dishes, *per se*, but are served in small quantities to complement the meal. Considerable invention goes into their creation and the Maharashtrians in particular are very proud of the diverse range of their pickles and chutneys. Pickles in the Indian sense are preserved chutneys, unlike the West, where no real distinction is made between pickles and chutneys.

Possibly this is because the Indian preserves brought into England by the East Indian merchants in the eighteenth century prompted brave attempts on the part of the English housewife to imitate them, but their failure to turn melons into mangos, and cucumber strips into bamboo shoots resulted in such extraordinary mixtures that they emerged as a totally new product, which they classified under the generic term pickle. Certainly these brave failures were the heralds of today's piccalilli. Small wonder they failed in their attempts, because many of the ingredients that go into the classic Indian preserved chutneys are almost impossible to get in the West. Not only that, some of them take weeks to prepare and involve very complicated procedures.

Together with the chutneys and/or pickles without which no Indian meal is complete, there are the side dishes proper. These are also carefully designed. Some are a variety of fruits and vegetables in yoghurt, called raitas, some are salads called salats, and others are mixtures of raw chopped vegetables with herbs, called cachumbars.

The recipes in this section cover some easily-prepared chutneys and a variety of side dishes. But they're only suggestions really. Some are standard, but this is one area where you unleash the epicurean imagination!

FRESH ACCOMPANIMENTS

Onion and Tomato Salad (Cachumbar)

2 medium onions, finely sliced
Salt
1 t vinegar or lemon juice

2 ripe firm tomatoes
Chopped coriander

Sprinkle the onions with salt and leave for 1 hour, then press out the liquid and rinse once in cold water. Combine all the ingredients and sprinkle with the coriander.

Eggplants in Yoghurt (Baigan Raita)

2 medium eggplants
1 c ghee
2½ c yoghurt
Salt

1 t ground cummin
1 t chopped fresh mint
Chilli powder to taste

Slice the eggplants and fry until golden. Set aside and cool. Beat the yoghurt with the cummin, mint, salt and chilli, then immerse the sliced eggplant in the mixture.

Eggplant Salad (Brihjal Salat)

2-3 medium eggplants
2 medium onions, finely chopped
1 fresh green chilli, seeded and finely chopped

1 T vinegar
2 T oil
1 t sugar
Salt

Cut the eggplants in half lengthways. Bake in a moderate oven (175°C)., for about 40 minutes until tender, then scoop out the pulp and mix well with all other ingredients. Chill for at least an hour before serving.

Yoghurt with Cucumber (Dahi Cachumbar)

3 medium cucumbers, finely sliced
Salt
1 c yoghurt
1 t fresh grated ginger
Fresh chopped coriander for garnish

2 medium tomatoes, peeled and chopped
1 fresh green chilli, seeded and chopped

Mix together first six items and sprinkle with chopped coriander.

Bananas and Yoghurt

4 large ripe bananas
1 fresh green chilli, seeded and
** chopped**
Salt

1 t garam masala
Chilli powder to taste
1 or 2 c yoghurt

Slice the bananas, then combine with all other ingredients. Sprinkle with coriander leaves.

Add in a little desiccated coconut if you wish, or try a chopped apple.

Onion Sambal (Piaz Sambal)

2 medium onions, sliced finely
A few mint leaves
1 t chilli powder, or to taste

1 t cummin seeds
Salt to taste
Juice of 1 lemon

Sprinkle the onion with the mint, chilli powder, cummin, salt and lemon juice. Toss all together.

Indian Salad (Cachumbar)

2 medium onions, finely chopped
3 tomatoes, peeled, seeded and
** chopped**
1 cucumber, peeled and chopped

1 seeded, chopped, fresh green chilli
Salt and fresh ground black pepper
White vinegar or tamarind water

Toss together first 5 ingredients and sprinkle with vinegar or tamarind water.

You can dress this with yoghurt instead of vinegar or tamarind water.

Banana with Coconut (Kela Chatni)

2 large bananas, chopped
½ c desiccated coconut

1 t ground cardamom

Mix together.

Sallets are a composition of edule plants and roots of several kinds to be eaten
raw or green, blanched or candied.
— John Evelyn, 1620-1706

SUNDRY PICKLES AND CHUTNEYS
WHICH CAN BE KEPT

Lemon Pickle

10 lemons
Juice of 5 more lemons
2 T salt

1 T turmeric
1 T garam masala

Cut lemons in small pieces and sprinkle with the salt and spices. Pour on the juice from 5 other lemons. Cover tightly and keep in a cool place for a week, shaking the jar every day. The pickle is ready when the skins are tender.

Sweet Cauliflower Pickle

1 large cauliflower
¼ c fresh grated ginger
2 T salt
1 T turmeric
Chilli to taste

1 T mustard seeds
1 T garam masala
1 T soft brown sugar
3 T vinegar
Juice of 1 lemon

Break the cauliflower into florets. Blanch in boiling water, then drain and cool. Sprinkle with the spices. Boil the vinegar, sugar and lemon juice together for a few minutes, then pour over the cauliflower. Mix well together and put in airtight jars. Keep in a warm place for a few days.

You can pickle other vegetables by this same method.

Mixed Vegetable Pickle

2 kg turnips or pumpkin
1 kg cauliflower
1 kg young carrots
500 g peas
4 cloves garlic
¼ c fresh grated ginger
¼ c chopped onions
600 ml sesame seed oil

1 T chilli powder
1 T garam masala
1 T mustard seeds
2 t turmeric
3-4 T salt
3 c vinegar
1 kg soft brown sugar

Peel and prepare all the vegetables. Slice the turnips or pumpkin and carrots and divide up the cauliflower into florets. Boil until they become tender but still firm. Remove and drain.

Grind up the garlic, ginger and onions into a paste, and fry. Cool, then mix with the vegetables. Put in jars and keep in a warm place for a few days. Boil up the sugar and vinegar, and pour over the vegetables. Keep in a warm place for a further two days. Keep tightly covered.

Lemon Achar

1 T mustard seeds
1 T black peppercorns
1 T fennel seeds
1 t cummin seeds

½ t chilli
1 t salt
6 lemons
1 cup mustard oil

Mix the spices and salt. Quarter the lemons and take out the pips. Put in jars and sprinkle with spices. Boil the oil and pour it over the lemons. Shake up well each jar and make it airtight.

Chilli Pickle

10 chillies
2 t salt
6 T lemon juice
Large dash asafoetida powder

4 t mustard seeds
1 t fennel seeds
2 t cummin seeds

Roast and grind spices. Split chillies lengthways and put the spice mix in them. Place in jars and pour over the lemon juice. Keep in warm place for a day. Shake this pickle up before serving.

Sweet Mango Chutney

1 kg half-ripe mangos
4 T salt
10 c water
4 T fresh grated ginger
6 cloves garlic, finely chopped

500 g sugar
2 c vinegar
½ t chilli powder
½ t garam masala
¼ c raisins

Peel and cube mangos. Make a brine from the salt and water, then soak mango in it overnight. Drain well and pat dry. In a heavy pan dissolve sugar and vinegar, bring to the boil and then simmer for 15 minutes. Add mangos, ginger and garlic and cook for another 15 minutes, stirring constantly. Now add the spices and raisins and continue cooking until the mixture thickens. Cool and transfer to airtight jars.

Mixed Fruit Chutney

2 large cooking apples
Same amount of pears
½ c dried apricots
2 T sultanas
¾ c soft brown sugar
1 c vinegar

1 t garam masala
12 cloves garlic, sliced
1 T fresh grated ginger
1 T salt
1 t carraway seeds or cummin

Peel and core the apples and pears. Cut all the fruit into small cubes. Mix the rest of the ingredients in a pan and add the fruit. Boil gently for about 30-40 minutes. Cool and transfer to airtight jars.

Tomato Chutney

4 large apples
2 kg tomatoes
4 T fresh grated ginger
2 T crushed garlic

Salt
1 t chilli powder
1 c vinegar

Peel and core apples. Cut into cubes together with the tomatoes. Pound together the garlic and ginger. Mix with the apples and tomatoes in a pan, sprinkle with salt and chilli powder and cover with vinegar. Cook until pulpy. Cool and bottle. You can add in a few raisins if you like.

Ginger and Garlic Chutney

2 c fresh grated ginger
¾ c garlic
2 T mustard seed
2 t chilli powder

2 t salt
1 c soft brown sugar
1 c vinegar

Grind ginger and garlic together. Mix with other ingredients and cook gently until the right texture is reached. Bottle when cool.

PICKLES AND CHUTNEYS

Sweets

Pageantry pervades all the panoply of Indian life. Festivals, holidays, weddings, births and birthdays — no excuse for celebration is overlooked. Despite the grinding poverty of a large part of the population — or perhaps because of it — the need for colour and pageantry is endemic and sweetmeats are a joyful feature of all these flamboyant festivals. Gilded with silver and gold leaf, they are symbols of extravagance, wealth and good fortune.

India has a sweet tooth and a dulcet item emerges somewhere in almost every meal: sometimes at the beginning to sweeten the mouth, occasionally in the middle of a meal as a foil to set off the spices, and even at the end — there is no fixed place.

There are literally hundreds of sweets in India. Some are simple and easily made, others require the specialised expertise of professional sweetmakers called Halvais, whose secret skills are passed on from father to son. These families of sweetmakers create their own regional masterpieces that are too time-consuming for the household cook to bother with. A sweet called Halva Sohan, for instance, requires wholewheat grains to be soaked for three or four days until the grain swells up, after which it is ground and a milky liquid squeezed out to be cooked with ghee, sugar and flavourings until the correct consistency is obtained. The fudge-like mixture is then shaped and topped with silver leaf, which is very difficult to apply because it is so fragile. It doesn't contribute to the taste at all, but it looks marvellous.

Many of these milk-based sweets are time consuming and tedious to make, because of the constant simmering and skimming that goes on to obtain the rich condensed milk that is essential to their creation.

The range of Indian desserts is staggering, and that is what a lot of us would be doing if we ate too many of them. Rich and creamy, or crunchy with layers of textures and flavours in a rainbow-hued assortment of colours, they are a source of sustenance to wrestlers and fairground strong men, but extremely dangerous to dieters. Some of the confections are almost too sweet, but the recipes which follow are only starting points and can be adjusted to suit the individual palate. Since most of us are not Halvais, I've kept the recipes simple, but satisfying — and perilous to the portly!

The fine arts are five in number — painting, poetry, music, architecture —
whose main branch is confectionery.
— Careme, 1783-1833

Mango Ice Cream (Kulfi Malai)

350 g tin condensed milk
1 ¼ c double cream
½ c granulated sugar
1 T grated almonds

1 T grated pistachios
350 g mangos, tinned, or mango pulp
1 T kewra water (or 2–3 drops of rose essence)

Boil the milk and cream together with the sugar, stirring constantly, then leave it to simmer on a low heat for 30 minutes. Next add the almonds and pistachios, stirring well, and leave to cool to room temperature by standing the pan in cold running water. Now add the mango and kewra water or rose essence. Combine the mixture well with a wire whisk and place to set in moulds. Use any shape you like, although the traditional Indian shape is conical. Place the moulds in a freezer and the ice cream will be ready when solid. Since this receipe contains no freezing agents, the ice cream melts quite quickly, so keep it in the freezer right up until serving.

Banana Ice Cream (Atul Kela Kulfi)

Proceed as for the Mango Ice Cream, but substitute **bananas** for the mango and add **1 t ground cardamom.**

Deep-fried Batter Coils (Jalebi)

Oil for deep frying
1 ½ c plain flour
½ c chickpea flour

7 g yeast
1 T yoghurt
1 ½ c lukewarm water

Syrup
2 c sugar
2 c cold water
½ t saffron powder

½ t ground cardamom
1 t orange food colouring

Mix the flours well. Soak the yeast in a little warm water for about 5 minutes to activate it, then dissolve it thoroughly. Add it to the flours, together with the yoghurt and lukewarm water and leave to ferment for about 2 hours. Meanwhile make the syrup. Heat the sugar and water until the sugar dissolves, then increase the heat and boil vigorously for 7 or 8 minutes, until the syrup is stringy. Just before it's ready, stir in the saffron, cardamom and colouring.

Heat up the deep-frying oil, and into this squeeze out the batter from either a funnel or a piping bag, in a series of little figure of eights or circles or what you will. Don't make them too thick. Fry, turning once, until a deep, rich gold, then remove with a slotted spoon and immerse in the syrup for about 3 minutes to allow the liquid to penetrate. Remove from the syrup and serve quickly as they lose their crispness if left too long.

Cream Balls in Syrup (Gulab Jamons)

½ c full-cream milk powder
3 heaped T self-raising flour
1 t baking powder
Pinch ground cardamom

3 T melted ghee
6 or 7 T water
Oil for frying
Syrup as for Jalebi (*See* p. 97)

Mix the milk powder with the flour, baking powder and a pinch of cardamom. Make a little hole in the centre and add the ghee and water. Blend into a stiff dough, pliable enough to be rolled into balls the size of walnuts or cocktail sausages. Deep-fry these balls until a rich golden colour, and remove. Either serve hot in the Jalebi syrup, or cold.

Cheese Balls In Syrup (Ras Gullas)

Panir made from 1200 ml milk (See
  Ingredients, p. 13, for recipe) or
  200 g commercial cottage cheese
1 t plain flour

Pinch bicarbonate of soda
Syrup as for Jalebi (*See* p. 97)
Rose water

Add the flour and bicarbonate of soda to the panir or cottage cheese and knead into a smooth dough. Roll and shape into small balls. When making the syrup, divide the mixture into 2 parts. Leave one aside, bring the other to boiling point and gently slip in the balls. Add a little water to the syrup and simmer for 10 minutes. When the balls float to the surface they are ready. Drain and put them in the remaining syrup. Drain, sprinkle with rose water and allow to stand for a minute or two before serving.

Pistachio Sweet (Pista Barfi)

1 c water
1 c sugar
1 c dried milk powder

8 crushed cardamoms
1 c pistachio nuts
Green food colouring

Make a syrup by dissolving the sugar in water then boiling briskly until the liquid thickens to a stringy consistency. Stir in the other ingredients, adding the colouring slowly to make it a light green. Spread out on a greased plate. Cut when cool.

Coconut Fudge (Narial Barfi)

A variation on the pistachio sweet above, not only in the ingredients but in the preparation.

½ c milk powder
1 c water
½ c sugar
2 heaped t ghee

4 heaped T desiccated coconut
1 t rose water (or 3 or 4 drops rose
  essence)

Make the milk powder into a smooth paste with $\frac{1}{2}$ c water. Prepare the syrup as for Jalebi way up to the stringy stage. Fry the coconut to a light gold, stirring well as it tends to stick. Add the milk paste to the syrup and stir in, then add the coconut and mix well. Stir until the mixture forms a lump and comes away from the sides of the pan. Add the rose water or essence and the cardamoms. Spread on a greased dish. Allow to cool before serving.

Ginger Sweet (Adrak Barfi)

3-4 T ghee
4 T semolina
$\frac{1}{2}$ c fresh grated ginger

$\frac{1}{2}$ c sugar
6 crushed cardamoms

Fry semolina and ginger until golden. Add the sugar and cardamom until the mixture becomes sticky. Turn on to a greased plate and let it cool.

Carrot Halva (Gajjar ka Halwa)

250 g carrots, prepared and grated
3 c milk
$\frac{1}{2}$ c sugar
6 crushed cardamoms

4 T ghee
2 T sultanas
Few blanched almonds

Cook the milk and carrots until it becomes almost a solid mass, stirring fairly often. (This can take a bit of time.) Add the sugar, ghee and sultanas and cook until the mixture starts to leave the side of the pan. Spread in a greased shallow dish. Sprinkle over the cardamoms and almonds.

Some people like to stir in a tablespoon or so of golden syrup when they add the sugar.

Banana Halva (Kela Halwa)

8 ripe bananas
1 c water

1 c sugar
Ghee

Boil and mash bananas. Make syrup in the normal way to the stringy stage, then add the bananas until it becomes a mass. Add the ghee slowly, stirring until the mass comes away from the sides of the pan. Turn on to a greased dish and allow to get cold.

Rice Pudding (Kheer)

⅓ c short-grain rice, washed and
    soaked for 30 minutes
4 c milk
3 cardamoms

12 raisins, soaked
⅓ c sugar
12 almonds
12 pistachios

Bring the milk to the boil and add the drained rice and the cardamoms. Bring to the boil again, then lower the heat and simmer, covered, until the rice is very soft. Stir in the raisins and sugar. Cook on a low heat until the pudding thickens slightly. Remove the cardamoms and pour into warmed glass dish. Allow to cool completely, garnish with the nuts and chill slightly before serving.

Vermicelli Pudding (Seviyan Kheer)

5 c milk
½ c broken vermicelli
⅓ c sugar
2 T sultanas

¼ c blanched slivered almonds
1 t rose water
1 T chopped pistachios

Bring the milk to the boil and add the vermicelli, stirring. Cook until the vermicelli is soft, then add the sultanas and almonds. Stir over a medium heat until the dish is the texture of custard. Add rose water and decorate with pistachios. Serve warm or chilled.

South Indian dancer

Drinks

It isn't unknown for those who wander abroad to be moved by curdled stomachs, and I think water may be the prime mover, either by being quaffed with gay abandon from beakers, or absorbed from droplets on salads and fruit and so forth. I am therefore chary of water as a drink even when it is suggested by experts as the only drink to take with curry. So, avoiding anything other than strong waters like the plague, unless from a well-engineered system or a mountain spring high above the pollution levels of pesticides, human and chemical fertilizers and bucolic hygienic practises, what do you drink with a curry?

A friend of mine is a descendant of the man who founded the famous Indian cavalry regiment of Skinners Horse, so who better, I thought, to ask this burning question. He appeared to ponder deeply and finally told me he would drink whatever was closest. A coarse military mind, I decided, and then thought again, because I've enjoyed a vast variety of drinks with Indian food, from lager to lassi and sharbet to champagne.

A few cautions, however. Full-bodied red wines are really wasted with highly spiced food, and ice-cold drinks often have the effect of turning up the heat. There are those who advise against bubbly drinks with curry, but one of the great sensations I've experienced was the divine balance of a well-chilled prickling champagne and a smooth hot Madras curry. Generally, full fruity wines and light Beaujolais-type reds go well with curry, and fruit punches similar to a Spanish sangria are quite splendid. Beers and lagers are all well thought of by bulk drinkers, but don't serve them too cold.

In the non-alcoholic area there is a parade of superb potions rejoicing in lovely names like faloodas, falsis, lassis and sharbet gulabs, and a religious beverage called bhang, prepared from the leaves of a certain hemp plant, which can give you a bit of a lift. Tea, of course, is drunk all over India, except in the south, where it is replaced by their magnificent coffee.

There is an interesting bit of Chinese mythology that accounts for the origin of tea. A weary Buddhist monk couldn't stop dozing off when he tried to concentrate on his meditation. To punish himself, he cut off his eyelashes. At the very spot where his lashes landed a tea plant sprouted. The monk took some of the leaves and brewed them up, using the miraculous tincture to refresh his jaded soul and keep himself awake. And thus the ubiquitous cup that cheers emerged to seduce the world. There seems little doubt that tea, in fact, did originate in China, and in many parts of the world, including India, the Chinese word chai is used for tea. The English char, as in 'cup of', is a military corruption of this ancient Chinese word. (I thought for a while that the term 'char lady' was an English variation on char wallah, but the term char in that sense is Shakespearean, from a verb of the period meaning to do a little job around the house.)

British Officers, Fourth Cavalry

TEA

There is only one tea plant, but there are many varieties yielding different flavours according to the location of the tea plantation. Tea leaves are basically of two types: the black fermented type, or the green unfermented variety. This distinction emerges from the treatment the leaves receive after they are picked. Most Indian tea is of the black persuasion, although some green tea is produced and drunk in Northern India. Green teas are traditionally brewed in water and served with or without sugar, but no milk. Black teas are also brewed in water or water and milk, already sweetened in India.

Chai

2 c water	**1 t black tea**
1 c milk	**Honey or sugar for sweetening to taste**

This will make 3 cups of tea. Keep the same proportions for greater or lesser amounts. The strength of the leaf is the only variable. Assam, Darjeeling and Ceylon teas are strong, and 1 heaped teaspoon will make 3 cups. Other teas or blends must be experimented with to get the strength.

Heat the milk and water to boiling point. (Poise yourself to remove it from the heat the instant it starts to boil.) Add the loose tea and cover tightly. Let it brew for a few minutes, stirring once. The tea is ready when it's a light orange colour.

You will get to know the brewing times of different teas. Always remove the tea leaves when the tea is brewed, otherwise it becomes bitter.

Masala Chai

Make as above, with the addition of **3 pinches of garam masala, 1 whole cardamom, 2 whole cloves** and **one small stick of cinnamon.**

Iced Tea

3 c cold water	**3 glasses iced water**
3 t loose black tea	**2 fresh lemons**
4 or 5 mint leaves	**Sweetening – sugar or honey to taste**

Boil 3 c water. Add the tea as before, with the addition of mint leaves if you like. Cover and brew, strain into a jug, and add the 3 glasses of ice-cold water, the lemon juice and sugar or honey to taste. Either refrigerate or pour into tall glasses with ice cubes. This makes 8-10 cups of iced tea. Delicious on a hot day.

Kashmir Chai

3 c water
1 t green tea

¼ t chopped ginger

Boil the water and pour over the green tea. Add ginger and cover. Brew for a minute or two and serve with honey.

Very good to combat indigestion.

TWO YOGHURT DRINKS

Lassi 1

1 c yoghurt or buttermilk
Sugar or honey to taste

1 c water
Drop or 2 of rose water

Beat yoghurt or buttermilk with the water until it has a smooth consistency. Pour into a tall glass with the crushed ice. Add the rose water and sweeten to taste.

Lassi 2

3 c buttermilk or yoghurt
Pinch salt
Ice cubes

1 c water
Pinch cummin powder

Blend the buttermilk or yoghurt with the water until it has a smooth consistency. Add some crushed ice and pour into a tall glass. Sprinkle over the salt and the cummin powder and mix well.

Hot Flavoured Milk (Garam Masala Doodh)

1 glass milk
1 whole clove
Sugar or honey to taste

1 cardamom pod
1 stick cinnamon

Heat but do not boil the milk. Add the whole uncrushed cardamom pod, together with the clove and the cinnamon. Let the mixture stand for a few minutes over a low heat, then remove pan from element, strain out the whole spices, sweeten to taste and serve.

Rose Sherbet (Sharbat Gulab)

2 c water
25 drops rose essence
2 t tulsi seeds (optional)

3 c sugar
1 t red food colouring
Crushed ice

Soak the tulsi seeds for a few minutes until they get a translucent covering over them. Dissolve sugar and water in a pan, then bring to the boil and cook until a thick syrup is obtained. Cool, add the rose essence and food colouring.

To serve, put about 2 T of the syrup in the bottom of a tall glass and top up with iced water and crushed ice. Add the tulsi seeds, stir and present.

Rose Milk Sherbet (Falooda)

Falooda is an exotic Indian version of the milkshake. There are many variations on this theme. Traditionally the drink should have particles of cornflour vermicelli floating in it, but these are difficult to make without special equipment, so substitutes are common. Tiny pieces of jelly, cooked tapioca or cornflour granules are frequently substituted.

Cornflour Granules

Heat a paste made of **cornflour** and **water** until it is a greyish colour. Cook for one more minute, then push it through a colander with small holes into **iced water,** where the little globules will set. You can make these in different colours with **food colouring.**

Agar Agar Jelly

3 c water
10 drops rose essence
4 t agar agar powder (or 1 c agar agar strands)

1 t red food colouring
6 T sugar
1 t green food colouring

If agar agar strands are used, soak them for at least 2 hours before commencing to make the jelly.
Measure water into pan, and sprinkle over agar agar powder. If using the strands, measure 1 loosely-packed cup of soaked strands. Bring to boil and simmer gently until the agar agar is dissolved. (Powder takes about 10 minutes, and the strands about half an hour.) Add sugar and dissolve, remove from heat, cool and then add the rose essence. Divide the mixture into two, and colour one green and the other red. Leave to set and then cut into strips and again into small dice.

The Sherbet

Agar agar jelly, or cornflour granules, or tapioca
Rose syrup as in Sharbat Gulab
(See above)

Crushed ice
Tulsi seeds (optional)
1 c ice-cold milk for each serving

Place 2 T each of the jelly and the rose syrup in each tall glass. Fill up with cold milk and crushed ice.

Almond Sherbet (Sharbat Badam)

2 c water
2¼ c sugar
1 T rose essence

4 T blanched almonds
8 ground cardamoms
Drop or 2 almond essence

Grind blanched and peeled almonds to a smooth paste. Mix with water, strain and add the sugar. Heat until the sugar dissolves and the mixture thickens. Add the cardamom, cool and add the rose and almond essences.

Mango Squash

Squashes are fresh fruit juices preserved in syrup.

2 c water
2 t citric acid
Orange or yellow colouring

2 c sugar
500 g mango pulp

Boil water, sugar and citric acid until the sugar dissolves and the syrup thickens. Cool. Pound or liquidise the mangoes. Stir in the colouring and mix it all through the liquid.

You can use the same amounts and the same principle with any fruits. Change the colourings, of course — unless you want a green orange drink or whatever.

A COUPLE OF ALCOHOLIC SUGGESTIONS

Sangria Punch

2 flagons red wine
8 c chilled orange juice
1 c brandy
½ c sugar dissolved in ½ c lemon juice
Ice

8 c soda water
Sliced oranges, apples and whatever
    else you have in the fruit line
    that looks pretty floating on the
    Sangria's surface

In a large bowl mix all your fruit slices plus the first 4 ingredients. At the last moment add the ice and soda water.

Orange Cup

2 c freshly squeezed orange juice
½ c brandy
Ice

½ c castor sugar
1 bottle champagne
Orange slices for garnish

Put orange juice and sugar in a large bowl. Stir and dissolve the sugar. Add the brandy and ice, pour over the champagne. Garnish with thinly sliced oranges.

Bhang

I include this as an historical anecdote only. Perish the thought that anybody would tamper with it in the West! This is a liquid infusion made from the leaves of a hemp plant called marijuana. It is drunk on religious occasions such as Shiv Ratri, to placate Lord Shiva, a quick-tempered god, in case he destroys the world with his third eye in a fit of pique. There is of course, a state-wide prohibition, but in Benares, considered to be the holiest place on earth by 600 million Hindus, this beverage is made every day in many of the temples, and is sold in stores and government shops.

2 c water
2 t marijuana (female leaves and
   flowers preferred)
4 c warm milk
2 T almonds, blanched and chopped

$\frac{1}{8}$ t garam masala
$\frac{1}{4}$ t powdered ginger
$\frac{1}{2}$ – 1 t rose water
Sweetening to taste

Boil water. Add the marijuana to the pot and cover. Brew for about 7 minutes. Strain the brew through a piece of muslin cloth and save the strained water. Squeeze the muslin containing the leaves and flowers to extract any remaining liquid. Add the collected liquid to the pot. Using a pestle and mortar, thoroughly grind the lump of leaves with about 2 t warm milk, and squeeze the liquid into the pot. Repeat this 4 or 5 times. Now add the almonds and a little more milk to the now pulpy mass in the mortar, grind into a fine paste and squeeze out the liquid. Repeat this until all that is left is some fibre and nut meal. Discard this and add to the liquids that have been collected, the garam masala, rose water and dried ginger. Add sugar or honey. Chill. Serve and seek Lord Shiva.

If you ever make this, do not enjoy it.

DRINKS

INDEX